The Synthesis
of Physics and Magic

a sketch of a unified world view

Table of Contents

A Consciousness

A   The Consciousness

There are several major themes that must be considered in depth in order to arrive at a unified world view – one of them is consciousness.

I   Two Views

The scientific worldview and the magical worldview are very different. However, while hardly any magician will deny the scientific research results and their technical application possibilities (most magicians have a driver's license …), the magical world view from the point of view of natural scientists is taken seriously only in rare cases.

As long as one has not had any experiences that clearly prove the existence of magical connections and effects, there is also no reason to take the magical world-view seriously. However, if one has both a driver's license and can telepathically retrieve a lost car key, at some point the need arises for a worldview that encompasses both aspects, science and magic.[1]

natural sciences and magic		
natural sciences	<== ???==>	magic

---

[1]   Short guidances to an easy and simple proof of telepathy, telekinesis and astrology may be found in my books „Telepathy for Beginners", „Telekinesis for Beginners" and „Astrology for Beginners".

I 1.   Physics and Magic

The basis of the natural sciences is physics. From it the laws of chemistry, biology, medicine, psychology, economy, ecology and politics are derived step by step – the science pyramid.

Magic has no such inner gradual order with a certain principle as a foundation, unless one would take will, imagination and analogies as this foundation. These three things appear in all magical, spiritual, occult and esoteric actions in different interpretation, evaluation and mixture.

In order to create a unified, i.e. uniform world view, which includes both the natural sciences and magic, it is therefore above all necessary to compare physics and magic – the other natural sciences can be left out for the time being to a large extent, since they are based on physics. However, evidences of magic may also be found in the other natural sciences.

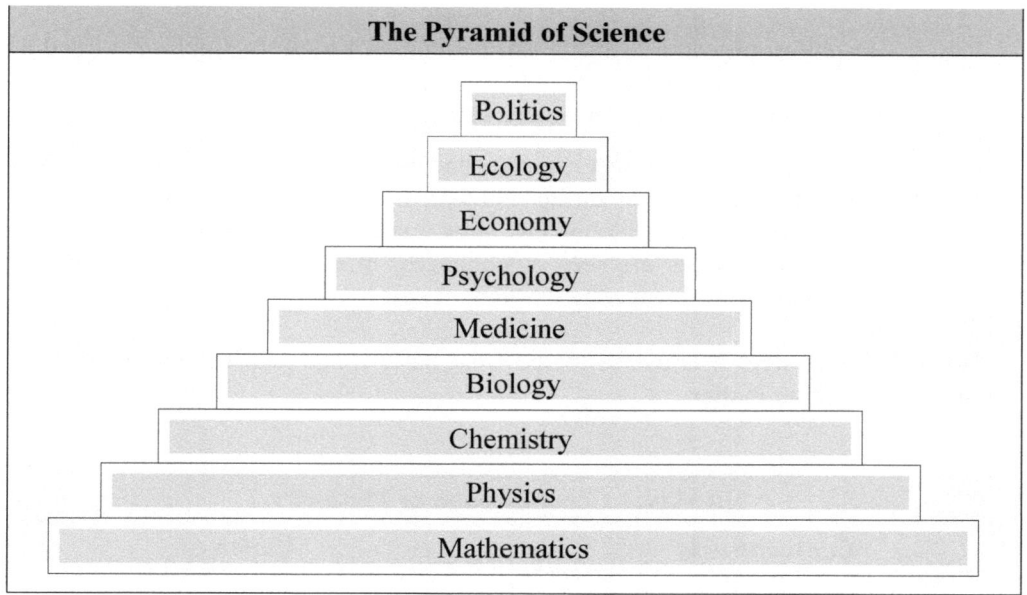

The Pyramid of Science

Politics
Ecology
Economy
Psychology
Medicine
Biology
Chemistry
Physics
Mathematics

I 2 Consciousness and Matter

The knowledge of physics results from the consideration of matter – the knowledge of magic, on the other hand, results from the consideration of the possibilities of actions of consciousness. From this follows that a unified world view must also clarify the question of the relationship between consciousness and matter in a convincing and plausible way.

Up to now, consciousness and matter stand side by side in our worldview somewhat without connection:

> - In the natural sciences, including psychology, consciousness is considered a side-effect of matter, which has no dynamics of its own – any structure and dynamics of consciousness, according to this view, results from the structure and dynamics of matter.
>
> Only C.G. Jung and Wilhelm Reich have conceived consciousness as something more independent. However, also they did not formulate a comprehensive model for the connection between consciousness and matter.

> - In philosophy and in mysticism the consciousness is usually regarded as the only real thing. The whole material world is from this view only a multiplicity of pictures in the own consciousness.

> - In religion, both consciousness and matter are seen as real, but their relationship is usually not further defined. In the monotheistic religions both are created by God, while in the older magic-mythological religions consciousness and matter are seen as connected in a pragmatic way because of the possibility to influence the world by magic.

Thus, as a first step, it is useful to see what basic things can be said about consciousness and about matter.

Reality: Consciousness or Matter?	
Consciousness	*Matter*
Philosophy/Mysticism	Science
Magic	

I 2. a)   Inside and Outside

The most obvious difference between consciousness and matter is that conscious-ness is inside and matter is outside.

The natural sciences regard the outside as real and see the inside as a consequence of the outside; philosophy and mysticism regard the inside as real and conceive the outside as an image within the inside; magic regards both as real, but is concerned almost exclusively with the possibilities of the inside influencing the outside.

From these three views important conclusions arise: The natural sciences always change states from the outside; philosophy, mysticism and magic always change states from the inside.

I 2. b)   Direct and Indirect Access

Closely connected with the "inside and outside" is the way of accessing the world, which is strikingly different in the various ways:

- If one acts from within, one has direct access: I can get up and get a glass of apple juice and drink it when I am thirsty. I can move my body directly from my consciousness.

- When you act from the outside, you have to move other things: I get a spade when I want to dig a hole to plant an apple tree – I can't get the earth out of the hole directly through my consciousness the way I can open my eyes, for example. Instead, I use my arms and hands, which I can move directly, to move the earth indirectly with them.

The area of the direct access is the own body – whereby the consciousness of a person can be differently well practiced to grasp the processes in the own body and also to move it according to the own imaginations.

- The matter becomes quite complex if one tries to get access to another human being, because this human being has of course also his own will and from this then possibly a battle of wills arises.

A mostly voluntary version of this attempt of a "hostile takeover" of another body by the will is hypnosis and especially remote hypnosis, where the hyp-notist and the hypnotized can be several miles apart.

- A large part of magic consists of extending the realm of direct access beyond one's own body – making thus the selected things on the outside an extended part of one's own body, so to speak.

Through this direct access to other people and things, telepathy, hypnosis and telekinesis become possible, as well as magic in the sense of directing chance.

I 2. c) Freedom and Determinism

The question "freedom or destiny" is one of the most discussed topics. To this question one can represent quite different points of view:

- Because physics considers the world as an interaction of almost infinitely many atoms, the physical world view describes the rules of this interaction of the atoms. This results in a deterministic view of the world: The properties of the particles involved in a process completely determine the process – if one knows everything about the current state of affairs, one can predict exactly how the state of affairs will develop.

- Mysticism starts from God, i.e. it derives the whole existence from God. Since God is the One-Only-All and there is no second besides Him, God is free – after all, there is nothing that could limit Him in any way.
From this it follows that every human being, if he succeeds in finding God in himself as his own origin, also attains this original freedom himself.

- Philosophy starts from the consciousness of man. The directions in philosophy, which regard the consciousness as the only real thing, ascribe also a perfect freedom to this consciousness, since it is the only real thing.

- Magic assumes that man can directly access external processes through his consciousness. The extent to which this is possible is estimated very differently by the different magical directions – and a very different extent of power is strived for.
One can also understand magic as the freedom from the laws of nature. Within the freedom/determinism opposition this "magic-freedom" arises from the fact that the magician has found the access to freedom.
Depending on the world view, this "inner freedom" that he has found again lies in himself or in God as the origin of all things.

The evaluation of the human freedom or non-freedom is estimated very differently depending on the world view.

There is also the aspect of this question that even in a world view in which everything is completely fixed, the own I (the own psyche) is a part of the world and consequently co-shapes the development of this world. Thus, even without perfect freedom, one has a formative influence on the world.

I 3.   Two Aspects of the Same World

In the development of a unified view of the world, one is confronted with the task of putting the two fundamental aspects of the world, i.e. consciousness and matter, into a coherent relation to each other.

I 3. a)   The Polarity

The considerations in the previous chapter have shown that there are several properties in which consciousness and matter differ from each other.

These differences are of great importance for the development of a unified world view:

Consciousness and Matter		
Subject	**Polarity**	
	Consciousness	*Matter*
place	inside	outside
access	direct access	indirect access
freedom	free	determined
knowledge	philosophy, mysticism, magic	physics, natural sciences

The world views, which result from the inside-centeredness or from the outside-centeredness, are very different – they are downright contradictory …

I 3. b)   A First Sketch

In order to arrive at a unified model, one can first make a sketch in which all known phenomena have a conclusive place. It is assumed that one has had enough experiences with magic to be sure that it really exists and is a real and effective possibility of action.

One can note several points that should be included in this first sketch of the unified worldview:

- <u>Matter acts on matter</u>: Rain falls on the earth and it becomes wet.

- <u>Matter acts on consciousness</u>: I see a car driving on the road and I wait to cross the road.

- <u>Consciousness acts on its own matter</u>: I move my arm and grab an apple.

- <u>Consciousness acts on foreign matter</u>: Telekinesis and "directing chance".

- <u>Consciousness acts on the own consciousness</u>: Thinking, self-knowledge, meditation, etc.

- <u>Consciousness acts perceptively on another consciousness</u>: Telepathy.

- <u>Consciousness acts perceptively on other matter</u>: Telepathy.

- <u>Consciousness has a formative effect on another consciousness</u>: Hypnosis and telekinesis.

- <u>Consciousness has a formative effect on other matter</u>: Telekinesis.

The basic idea, by which one can bring these phenomena into a uniform picture, is that consciousness and matter are two sides of the same thing. This means that the inside corresponds to the outside.

This is at least a plausible approach, since it is undoubted that a human being has both a body and a consciousness and both are closely connected with each other.

In the following sketch the different processes have been considered from person 1 on the left side.

Sketch: "Inside = Outside"			
consciousness 1		telepathy, hypnosis →	consciousness 2
		telekinesis →	→→→→→↓
own action ↓	↑ own perception		telekinesis ↓
matter 1		physical effect →	matter 2

Telekinesis appears in this first sketch as an extension of one's consciousness to the object one wishes to move. Since the object thereby becomes temporarily an extension of one's own body, so to speak, one can then move it. Telekinesis therefore has two arrows: "Consciousness 1 → Consciousness 2 → Matter 2."

Of course, this first sketch does not explain much yet – it is first of all only the attempt to summarize all observed phenomena in a simple graph.

II The Transition
between Consciousness and Matter

The interesting point of the previous considerations is of course the transition between consciousness and matter. What happens there? What is possible there? What structures and dynamics can be found there?

This area has not yet been explored too thoroughly.

II 1. „Inside = Outside"

What happens between inside and outside, between direct and indirect access, between freedom and determinacy? There the inside reaches the outside, there the individual reaches the general and there the free reaches the formed … this seems to be an inventive, creative, artistic process.

Inside is the vision, the desire, the will – outside is the created, the result, the object. This transition seems to be what life is all about: the independent creation of one's own life, self-determination, self-development.

If there were only the inside, there would be no experience of oneself in the world. If there were only the outside, there would be only unconscious machines. But since there are both and both are connected with each other, there is also magic, which seems to be essentially a creative act.

Inside = Outside
inside: consciousness (free, direct access)
transition: consciousness and matter are coupled to each other
outside: matter (determined, indirect access)

II 2. The Life Force

The transition area between consciousness and matter is experienced and described as "life force". Mostly this force is perceived as a misty substance, which can be seen optically as a milky white mist with a slight blue shimmer and which can be felt by the body as warmth and heat and as a slight electric tingling.

These perceptions do not mean that there is a milky-white and warm life-force – they only mean that consciousness perceives this transition between consciousness and matter in this form, i.e. that consciousness translates this transition into these optical and thermal images to give them a shape.

On the one hand, this life force is shaped by the matter to which it belongs – but on the other hand, it is also shaped by the consciousness to which it belongs. The imprinting of the life force by the consciousness is what constitutes a large part of magic. The two tools in this process are concentration and imagination – directing one's will to the image of what one wants to achieve. Concentration or will is the focus of consciousness, its direction – the imagined image is a content of consciousness, the goal of the will.

When consciousness wants to form matter, or even to move one's own body, it does so by aligning itself with the desired goal – whether that is getting up from a chair, summoning a relationship by magic, or telekinetically moving a feather.

Vital Force
Inside: consciousness (free, direct access)
Transition: "life force" (coupling of consciousness and matter to each other)
Outside: matter (determined, indirect access)

II 3.   The Stage Models

There are many models describing the path from matter to consciousness – generally these descriptions come from the different directions of mysticism and are presented in the form of a path from earth to God.

II 3. a)   The Tree of Life

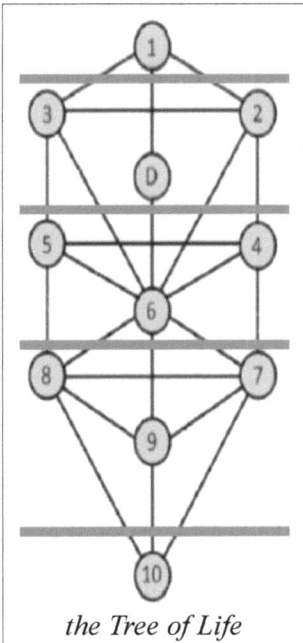

the Tree of Life

The Tree of Life from the Kabbalah, i.e. from Jewish mysticism, is a system of 11 sections, 22 connections, 3 triangles between these sections as well as 4 transitions between the individual sections in this graphic.

This rather complex system is an inherently logical form that can be derived from simple basic principles.

Therefore, this 40-part structure can be found in all things as an internal structure – starting with a single-celled organism and a human being over a vacuum cleaner and a car up to the German constitution and evolution as a whole.

This system has been conceived as a "way to God", but it is universally applicable.[2]

The main five stages of this path are:

> God (in the diagram: "1")
> Gods (in the diagram: "D")
> Soul (in the diagram: "6")
> Life Force (in the diagram: "9")
> Body (in the diagram: "10"),

These five levels are also called "Middle Pillar".

The mentioned four transitions lie between these five areas (in the diagram: gray crossbars).

---

2   A detailed description may be found in my three books „Blüten des Lebensbaumes I, II, III".

II 3. b)   The Middle Pillar

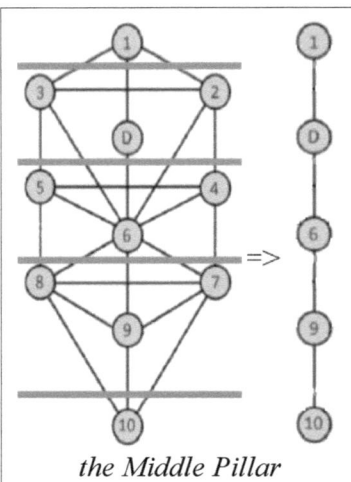

the Middle Pillar

The Middle Pillar is a meditation or ritual derived from the Tree of Life that takes into account only the five basic sections: Body, Life Force, Soul, Gods, God. They correspond to the middle of the three pillars of the Tree of Life graphic.

These five sections are imagined as colored shining spheres in the body:

- a white sphere above the head, i.e. at the crown chakra (1 = God);
- a rainbow-colored sphere in the neck/head (D = Gods);
- a golden sphere in the chest, i.e. in the heart chakra (6 = Soul);
- a violet sphere in the abdomen (9 = Life Force);
- and a brown sphere under the feet, i.e. under the foot chakras (10 = Body).

II 3. c)   The Rose Path

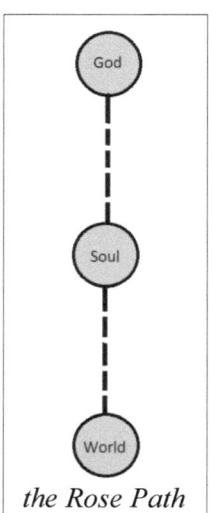

the Rose Path

The Rose Path is the equivalent of the Tree of Life in Islamic mysticism. It, too, begins with the body and ends with God, and on it, too, one meets one's own soul halfway.

The Rose Path is less systematically structured than the Tree of Life and there are several versions of it. These versions differ mainly in the number of individual steps on this two-part path.

II 3. d) The Lamrim

Buddhism also has such a "mystic map". Its name translates as "step-way". Its beginning is again the body, its end, however, is enlightenment ("Nirvana"), because in Buddhism there is no supreme deity.

Since Buddhism emphasizes the impermanence of the soul, its midway realization is not specially accentuated.

II 3. e) Visions

The five basic realms on the path from matter/body to consciousness/God are experienced distinctly differently. The nature of their visual perception is also easily distinguishable with a little practice.

Since these differences might be helpful in an understanding of the relationship between consciousness and matter, they are described here in more detail:

The Stages of the Path on the "Middle Pillar"		
Stages	*Name*	*Perception*
God	Kether	non-divided, glistening white light or shining blackness
transition	*last step*	*upwards: coming to rest, fullness (unity)* *downward: impulse of creation ("storm of light")*
deities	Da'ath	contours in the light; no demarcations, but different qualities
transition	*abyss*	*widening of perspective, dissolution of all delimitations*
soul	Tiphareth	luminous from within, mostly unmoving images
transition	*trench*	*very sharp contours; shining from inside; constantly flowing forms*
life force body	Yesod	colourless or only slightly colored contours in a general, slightly luminous mist
transition	*threshold*	*becoming still, turning inward, feeling something*
body	Malkuth	normal external optical perception with the eyes

As a new element, it becomes clear here that matter is differentiated and consists of many individual elements which are separated from each other (outer perception), while consciousness is a unity (glistening white, not divided light).

The soul in the middle between these two endpoints of the path has properties of both: on the one hand, it is differentiated and has different qualities, and on the other hand, it is connected with many other things.

II 3. f)   The Forms of Consciousness

If one wants to understand the nature of consciousness, it is helpful to consider also the different forms in which consciousness can appear.

- The best known is certainly the waking consciousness, which is reading these lines right now. This consciousness coordinates the contents of consciousness that are relevant to the momentary situation – all other perceptions and memories are blocked out.

The waking consciousness is like an office, diligently working on the current tasks.

- Then there is the subconscious, which can be experienced in dreams. In it are all the perceptions and memories of the relevant person.

The subconscious, which is also called dream consciousness, it is like a large, well-organized archive.

- Further, there is the ecstatic state, which will be known to most primarily as orgasm and as panic. This consciousness is focused on a single object.

This consciousness is like a bright office desk lamp that illuminates only one thing – that which is existentially important at the moment.

- Finally, there is the deep sleep consciousness, which will be the most unknown – simply because it is consciousness itself without content to look at. The direct perception of this consciousness is possible above all in the silence meditation, in which only the consciousness is there, which is conscious of itself, but has no other contents.

The deep sleep consciousness is like the paper on which all the contents of consciousness are painted.

The deep sleep consciousness is like a house; the subconsciousness is like an archive in that house; the waking consciousness is like an office in that house that has access to the archive; the ecstasy consciousness is like the lamp on the desk in that office that intensely illuminates a single thing.

- Then there is the collective subconscious. This is the telepathic linking of the archives of all the houses in a city, that is, the subconsciousness of all the people together.

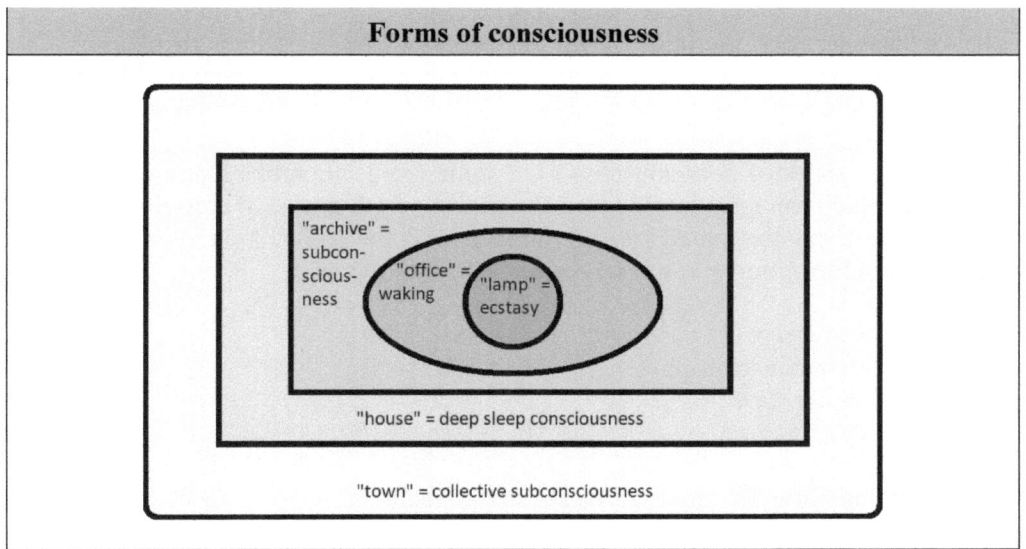

Forms of consciousness

"archive" = subconsciousness

"office" = waking

"lamp" = ecstasy

"house" = deep sleep consciousness

"town" = collective subconsciousness

These forms of consciousness correspond to the lower three sections of the Middle Pillar, i.e. the path from the body to the soul and thus the first half of this path, which is in man himself.

- The waking consciousness corresponds on the Middle Pillar to Malkuth, that is, the everyday consciousness, the body, the matter, the "normal" optical perception of the world.
- The ecstasy consciousness is not listed separately on the Middle Pillar – it is an aspect of Malkuth.

- The dream consciousness corresponds on the Middle Pillar to Yesod, i.e. the life force, the psyche, the astral body, the misty inner perception of the world.
- The collective subconsciousness consists of the telepathically coupled

21

subconsciousnesses of the individual people.

- The deep sleep consciousness corresponds on the Middle Pillar to Tiphareth, that is, to the soul, to the perception of simple images and symbols that shine from within and that usually do not move.

In meditation different forms of consciousness are coupled with each other:

waking consciousness + subconsciousness	= dream journey
waking consciousness + deep sleep consciousness	= silent meditation
waking consciousness + ecstasy consciousness	= Kundalini meditation
all four states of consciousness	= mandala meditation

The known states of consciousness have some more properties like a certain EEG frequency, which can be measured when a person is in that state of consciousness.

These electrical frequencies in the brain (EEG) have a striking regularity – the frequency doubles from one state of consciousness to the next:

- Deep sleep:	2 - 4Hz ≈ 3Hz
- dream consciousness:	4 - 8Hz ≈ 6Hz
- Waking state:	8 - 16Hz ≈ 12Hz
- Ecstasy:	16 - 32Hz ≈ 24Hz

In meditation, these frequencies are blended together:

- two vibrations of ecstasy into one vibration of waking consciousness.

- two vibrations of the waking consciousness into one vibration of the dream consciousness

- two vibrations of the dream consciousness into one vibration of the deep sleep consciousness.

This "fitting things together" is also the basic feeling when striving for a meditative state – and the feeling when reaching this state is a greater inner order and harmony.

In the following overview the "wavelengths" of the different modes of consciousness are shown – once uncoordinated as in normal consciousness and once fully coordinated as in deep meditation.

A frequency twice as high corresponds to a wavelength half as long – a tone twice as high has a frequency twice as high and a wavelength half as long.

The coordination of the rhythms of consciousness in meditation

uncoordinated rhythm (normal consciousness)

deep sleep		
dream				
waking								
ecstasy																	

coordinated rhythm (meditation)

deep sleep		
dream				
waking							
ecstasy															

The transitions between the uncoordinated forms of consciousness form thresholds of consciousness – one consciousness has no direct access to the other because it vibrates differently. Through rhythm, mantras, chanting, concentration and similar methods, the rhythms of the consciousness are attuned to each other, whereby the threshold of consciousness dissolves and the consciousness can expand. Thus, mediation is simply the creation of resonance between the vibrations of two forms of consciousness.

According to the way from matter (body) to the comprehensive consciousness (God), which is described among others by the Middle Pillar, there would have to be two more forms of consciousness, which correspond to the realm of the deities ("Da'ath") and the realm of unity or God ("Kether").

In the following overview, the most important characteristics of all these states of consciousness are listed once again:

The Stages of the Path on the "Middle Pillar"					
Stages	*Name*	*Consciousness*	*Number of contents of the consciousness*	*Frequency*	*Perception*
God	Kether	(oneness with God)	(everything)	0.75hz (?)	glistening white light or shining blackness
transition	*last step*				*upwards: coming to rest, fullness ("unity"); downward: creation impulse ("light storm")*
Deities	Da'ath	(invocation of a deity)	(all in relation to one deity)	1.5hz (?)	contours in the light, no delimitations, but different qualities
transition	*abyss*				*widening of perspective, dissolution of all boundaries*
Soul	Tiphareth	deep sleep consciousness	no	3 hz	glowing from within, mostly motionless images
transition	*trench*				very sharp contours, glowing from inside, constantly flowing forms
life-force-body	Yesod	dream-consciousness	all in the psyche	6hz	colorless or only slightly colored contours in a general, slightly luminous fog
		collective sub-consciousness	all of one human group		
transition	threshold				to become still, to turn inward, to feel something
body	Malkuth	waking-consciousness	the relevant ones in the situation	12hz	normal external optical perception with the eyes
		ecstasy	one	24hz	

These considerations to the transition from matter to consciousness show several things at once:

- The transition is not a sharp border, but a differentiated area, at which detailed processes take place.

- The transition is continuous and can be subdivided into steps as among other things the regular frequency changes from one state of consciousness to the next as well as the gradual development of the forms of perception show.

This "continuity divided into steps" already results from the fact that 1. consciousness and matter affect each other – so there must be a firm connection between both, and that 2. consciousness and matter are different and therefore there must be a "systematic transition" between them.

- Where you are on this transition determines how you see the world:

- Kether: world = God/unity
- Da'ath: world = deities
- Tiphareth/deep sleep consciousness: world = souls
- Yesod/subconsciousness: world = life Force
- Malkuth/waking consciousness: world = matter

- It can be assumed that the place where one is on this transition, i.e. the state of consciousness one can reach with his waking consciousness, also determines the degree of freedom one has:

- Kether: completely free
- Da'ath: "extraordinary" magic (miracle)
- Tiphareth/deep sleep: resting in oneself
- Yesod/subconsciousness: "ordinary" magic
- Malkuth/waking consciousness: completely determined

- Finally, the way from matter (earth, Malkuth) to consciousness (God, Kether) is also "widening of consciousness" – strictly speaking a widening of the contents of consciousness, which are attainable for the consciousness:

- Kether: unity (without differentiation)
- Da'ath: everything
- Tiphareth/deep sleep: everything that belongs to the soul
- Yesod/subconsciousness: contents of the psyche and telepathy
- Malkuth/waking: situation

25

These considerations show that the transition from matter to consciousness is a complex process:

The transition from consciousness to matter			
	Matter	*Transition*	*Consciousness*
differentiation	multiplicity	differentiation	unity
continuity	multiplicity	continuity	unity
contents	many	gradual differentiation	one
world view	God	soul	world
degree of freedom	free	increase of magical possibilities	determined
EEG frequency	≈ 24Hz	≈ 12Hz / 6 Hz / 3Hz / 1,5 Hz (?)	≈ 0,75Hz (?)

A question arises in the considerations in this section, because an inconsistency has occurred therein: From ecstasy and waking consciousness (Malkuth) to life force (Yesod), soul (Tiphareth) and deities (Da'ath) to Kether (God) there is a gradual increase in the number of contents of consciousness – only the soul falls out of this sequence:

- unity   = all encompassing consciousness
- all contents of one deity   = boundaryless consciousness
- the soul   = deep sleep, inner silence
- all contents of the psyche   = dream
- the situation-relevant contents = waking
- one content   = ecstasy

One should actually assume that the soul contains all memories of its previous incarnations as well as its intentions for its present incarnation. This is true – one can find these contents of consciousness on dream journeys and in meditations in one's soul (Tiphareth).

The emptiness of the deep sleep consciousness, i.e. the soul consciousness, is therefore only a phenomenon that one experiences when one enters this consciousness from the psyche – the contents of the psyche fall silent, which is why this consciousness appears as empty. However, if one looks there more closely, one can find the contents of the consciousness of the soul, which, however, lie beyond the framework of one's own present life and are therefore not so easily accessible.

II 3. g) Thresholds of Consciousness

There is a striking phenomenon, which is hardly noticeable, however, because this is completely "normal": Not everything is accessible to the consciousness in the normal state. Consciousness is limited in terms of the contents it can perceive.

Why actually? If it is really free by its nature, it should also be able to perceive all things (telepathy) and to direct all things (telekinesis).

First of all one can distinguish two things: the consciousness itself and its contents. Moreover, the quality of consciousness itself depends on the kind of contents of consciousness: without contents = deep sleep; all contents = dream; the situation-relevant contents = waking; one content = ecstasy.

So there must be something third that shapes the nature of consciousness: some kind of threshold of consciousness. This presumed group of thresholds of consciousness probably correspond to the transitions on the Middle Pillar, which separate the different kinds of consciousness on it.

Meditation is the crossing of one of these thresholds of consciousness. As already shown, it means that the rhythms of two modes of consciousness are tuned to each other.

> Waking consciousness + dream consciousness = dream journey;
> Waking consciousness + deep sleep = silence meditation;
> Waking consciousness + ecstasy = Kundalini meditation.

In meditation, the frequency of one state of consciousness (waking) is coordinated with the frequency twice as high (ecstasy) or with the frequency half as high (dream) or with the frequency a quarter as high (deep sleep) of another state of consciousness. Thus, a unified, complex pattern of vibration is achieved: a tone and its higher or lower octave.

The range of consciousness obviously depends on which forms of consciousness have been coordinated with each other with regard to their frequencies.

From this it follows again that the boundaries of consciousness are simply frequencies which have not been tuned to each other.

Here again is the diagram showing the effect of meditation on the rhythms of consciousness:

27

The coordination of the rhythms of consciousness in meditation																
uncoordinated rhythm (normal consciousness)																
deep sleep																
dream																
waking																
ecstasy																
coordinated rhythm (meditation)																
deep sleep																
dream																
waking																
ecstasy																

It seems as if there is a high order in the realm of consciousness, which seems almost mathematical and geometrical.

If consciousness is closely connected with matter and matter is characterized by the laws of physics and mathematics, traces of this should also be found in consciousness.

Strictly speaking, of course, these should not be traces, but rather roots, since a gradual transition should be found between the two opposites of the determinacy of matter and the freedom of consciousness.

II 3. h)   The Position of the Soul

In the previous considerations, within the "normal" four human states of consciousness (ecstasy, waking, dream, deep sleep), the soul is connected with the root of these four forms of consciousness: with deep sleep, with the contentless consciousness which is conscious only of itself.

At the same time, however, the soul is also the middle of the path between matter and consciousness, i.e. between the whole matter (world) and the all-embracing consciousness (God).

If the previous assumption is correct that consciousness and matter are only two sides of the same thing, all things have a consciousness. The contents of this consciousness depend on the complexity of the considered thing: a human being, an animal, a plant, a whole plant species, a stone, a mountain, a sea, a planet etc.

The consciousness of some of these things has been given a name throughout history: Man – consciousness; animal – animal spirit; plant species – elf; all wolves – wolf goddess; earth – earth goddess; sea – sea god; all people – collective subconscious; the whole earth with all living beings on it – Gaia; etc.

Ecstasy, waking, dream and deep sleep are the four individual forms of consciousness. They correspond on the Middle Pillar to Malkuth (body = waking and ecstasy), Yesod (dream = life force) and Tiphareth (deep sleep = soul).

Furthermore there are two general forms of consciousness. They correspond on the Middle Pillar to Da'ath (delimitation = deities) and Kether (unity = God).

The deities are a differentiation of the one God. A soul is a "drop" from the "sea" of one of these deities. A life force body and therefore a psyche is the sum of the experiences of a soul in one of its incarnations. The body is the material form that the life force takes at a given moment.

Here, too, we find a gradual, continuous differentiation from unity to multiplicity. This sequence "God – divinity – soul (deep sleep) – dream state (subconsciousness) – waking – ecstasy" can also be represented as a "map":

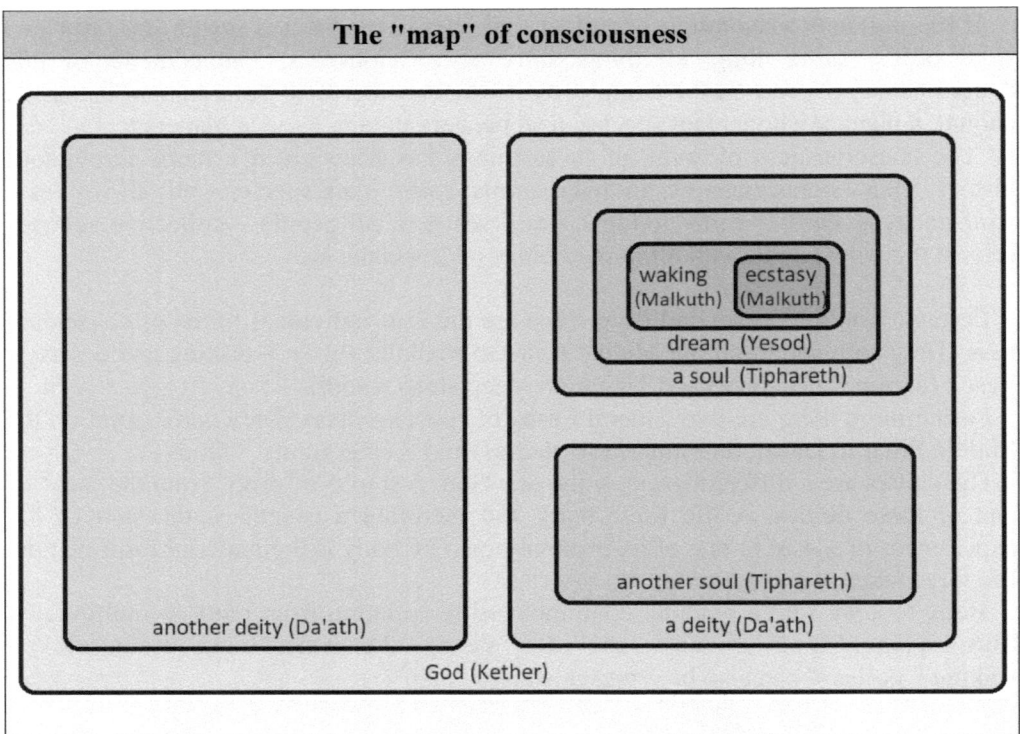

The "map" of consciousness

waking (Malkuth) ecstasy (Malkuth)

dream (Yesod)

a soul (Tiphareth)

another soul (Tiphareth)

another deity (Da'ath) a deity (Da'ath)

God (Kether)

The position of the soul in the middle between the one, all-embracing consciousness and the differentiated matter, which is subdivided into single elements, lets assume that the soul is the inventive, creative element. It should have both freedom (the quality of consciousness) and the possibility of concretization and determination (the quality of matter).

II 3. i) Planetary Sequence

Another sequence, very similar to the step paths considered so far, is the astrological planets: Moon, Mercury, Venus, Sun, Mars, Jupiter, Saturn, Uranus, Neptune and Pluto.

But this is not an independent sequence, because it can look different in every solar system – and even in our own solar system one could include the minor planets Ceres, Eris, Sedna, Makemake, Haumea etc. in this sequence.

30

However, the above-mentioned planetary sequence, together with the Earth as the starting point, appears as one of the many assignments to the Kabbalistic Tree of Life. The five areas of the Middle Pillar are underlined:

<u>Kether</u>	- <u>Pluto</u>
Chokmah	- Neptun
Binah	- Uranus
<u>Da'ath</u>	- <u>Saturn</u>
Chesed	- Jupiter
Geburah	- Mars
<u>Tiphareth</u>	- <u>Sun</u>
Netzach	- Venus
Hod	- Mercury
<u>Yesod</u>	- <u>Moon</u>
<u>Malkuth</u>	- <u>Earth</u>

II 3. j) Summary

Consciousness appears in the previous considerations as the "inside" of the same thing whose outside appears as matter – consequently all things have consciousness.

The transition from consciousness to matter is 1. continuous, it is 2. divided into several steps, it represents 3. a fixed connection, it is 4. a transition from the freedom of consciousness to the determinacy of matter and it is 5. thus the creative and magical realm.

The kind of consciousness depends on how close it is to matter. The kind of consciousness depends also an the contents, with which it is connected.

The expansion of the waking consciousness to a larger realm is obtained by integrating the frequency of the waking consciousness with the frequency of another consciousness that is a lower octave of the waking consciousness frequency (dream, deep sleep) or a higher octave (ecstasy). This is usually done through meditation.

The transitions between the different types of consciousness, i.e. the thresholds of consciousness, occur because the frequencies of the two types of consciousness have often not been coordinated with each other.

II 4. The Tube Model

It would be helpful at this point of the considerations to have a model which summarizes the previous results in a clear way. A model is of course not yet a "photo" of reality, but if a model can describe all observations precisely, this is already a great help for further research.

II 4. a) The Feynman Diagrams

The American physicist and Nobel laureate Richard Feynman (1918-1988) developed a method to illustrate processes in the field of quantum physics. This method is used today by almost all physicists. Feynman received his Nobel Prize among other things also for the development of this representation method.

Since these diagrams work so well and simply, it could be helpful to use them in the sketching of a unified magical-physical model.

These diagrams illustrate any physical processes even at the level of elementary particles. Such a diagram may look like the following:

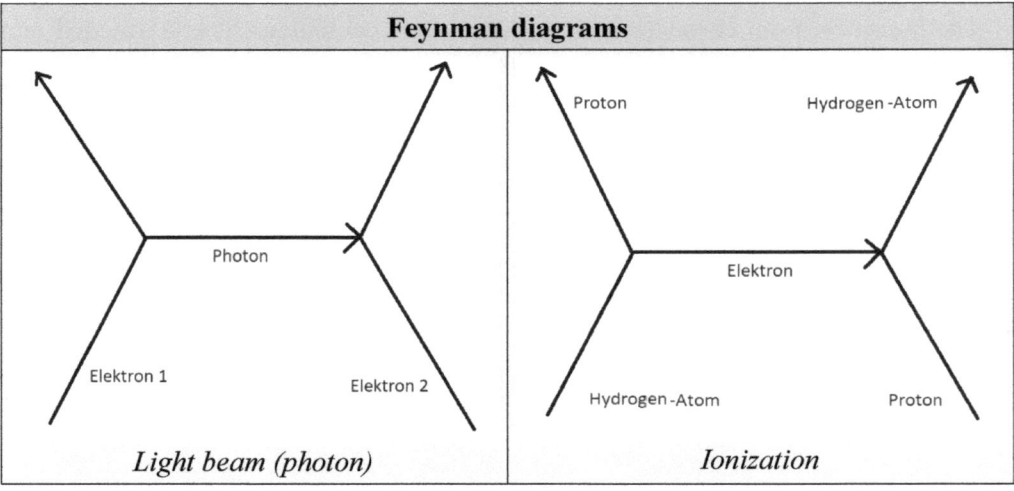

In the left diagram two electrons fly from the bottom to the top. Since they both have a negative electric charge, there is an electric repulsion between them, which can be represented as a photon (= particle of the electromagnetic force) flying from electron 1 to electron 2. Since electron 1 emits a mass (the photon) to the right, its trajectory bends to the left (law of conservation of momentum). Electron 2, on the other hand, is hit from the left by the mass of the photon, whereupon its trajectory bends to the right.

The diagram on the right shows a hydrogen atom and a proton. A hydrogen atom consists of a proton and an electron. When the hydrogen atom gives up its electron to the proton, the hydrogen atom turns into a proton, while the proton turns into a hydrogen atom by accepting the electron. A proton can also be thought of as an ionized, or electron-less, hydrogen atom – hence the diagram on the right shows the ionization of the left one of the two atoms.

In these two diagrams, time proceeds from bottom to top. However, all these diagrams can also be read with time running from top to bottom – in that case, on the right diagram, a hydrogen atom is formed on the left side and a proton on the right side.

These diagrams show, among other things, that all physical processes can be represented as exchange processes: Everything that happens is an exchange of particles.

This in turn means that for each particle, one can see how it moves through time, exerting an effect on other particles through the exchange of particles and receiving an effect from the other particles themselves.

If one thinks through this picture systematically and relates it to all processes in the world, one obtains an inconceivably large quantity of trajectories of particles which all act on each other by the exchange of particles: There are only these trajectories of particles which are all constantly connected with all other particles by the exchange of particles.

The whole world is nothing else than a huge quantity of such particles flying through space and time, which constantly exchange smaller particles with each other …

The particles which are exchanged are mostly gravitons, photons and gluons, i.e. the energy quanta of gravity and of electromagnetic force and of color force inside atomic nuclei.

Consequently, the world is a big net of "threads" (the trajectories of the particles) which are constantly connected with each other. There is only this one particle net – and everything that exists is part of this net.

If one looks at the world only at a single point of time, one sees single particles which are at a certain place in time and in space – so looked at, each particle is isolated from all other particles.

If you look at the world in the flow of time, there are only the "particle threads" which are connected to all other particles by "exchange particle threads" – there is only the one big net.

Also in the following representation of a tiny section from this "particle net" the time runs from the bottom to the top. The lines show the trajectories of the particles (lines diagonally upwards) and their interactions (horizontal lines).

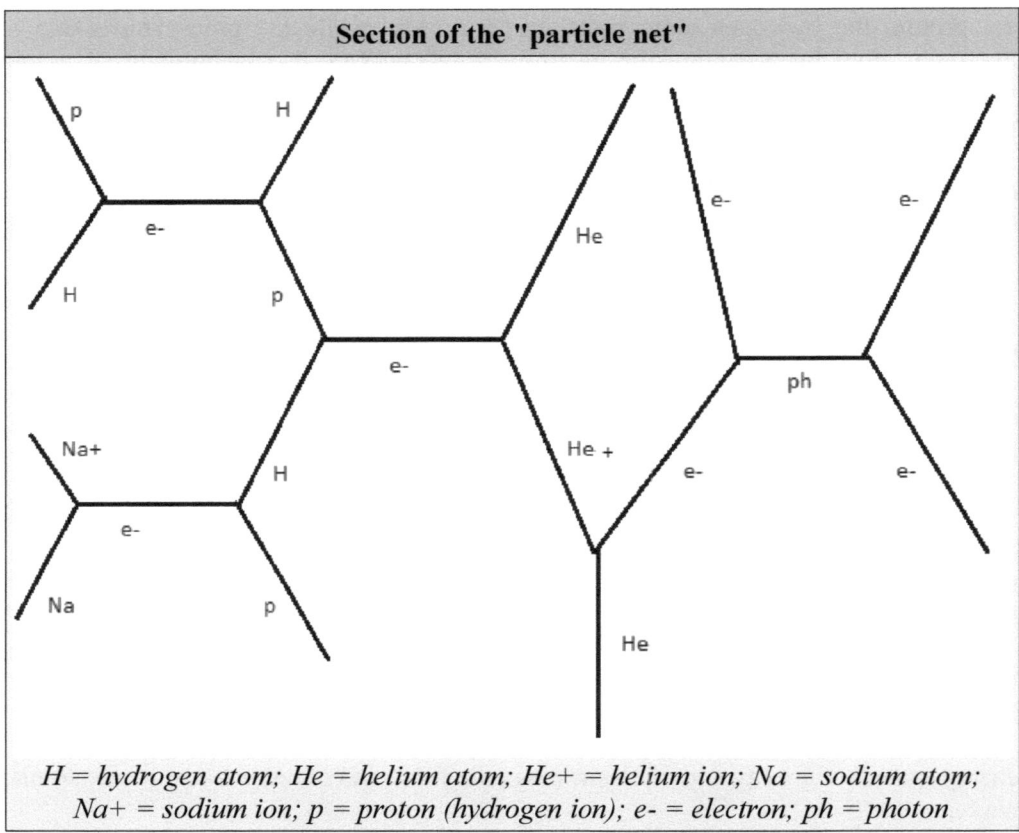

Section of the "particle net"

H = hydrogen atom; He = helium atom; He+ = helium ion; Na = sodium atom; Na+ = sodium ion; p = proton (hydrogen ion); e- = electron; ph = photon

Everything that is in the world and that happens in the world can be represented as such a net – in the end, of course, there is only one, all-encompassing net.

Everything is connected with everything.

II 4. b)   The Superstring Theory

The second element from physics, which is very useful for the development of a unified model, are the superstrings. They are the present unified mathematical description of all the particles that make up our world.

This description represents the particles as oscillating circles. The particles are like a vibrating string, which is not stretched straight like a string of a violin, but forms a circle.

When such a particle vibrating as a circle moves through space, it is no longer a "string-circle" but a "tube". The "net" thus becomes a tube system, a "tube net".

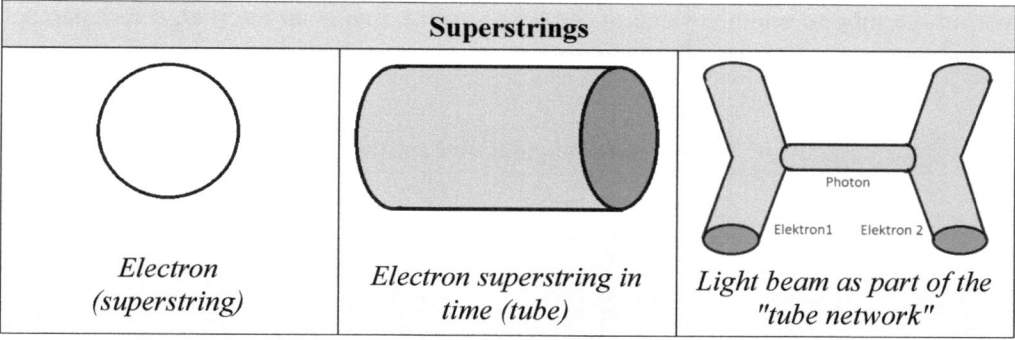

Superstrings		
Electron (superstring)	*Electron superstring in time (tube)*	*Light beam as part of the "tube network"*

So, if you describe the world using two of the most important ways of representing physics today, you get a picture of the world that resembles a complex system of tubes.

God is a plumber …

II 4. c)   Inside and Outside

The fundamental problem in the previous considerations was the simultaneous existence of consciousness and matter and thus the question of the relation between these two.

Matter appears as the outside of the world and consciousness as the inside of the world. The image of the tube system offers a simple graphic representation of this opposition: the outside of the world (matter) is the outside of the tubes – the inside of the world (consciousmess) is the inside of the tubes.

In this model, everything has an outside and is thus matter – and everything also has an inside and thus has consciousness. The complexity of the contents of the consciousness corresponds to the complexity of the tube system to which this consciousness belongs (a stone, a flower, a man etc.).

From this picture also results that there is on the one hand an inner perception and an action from the inside, thus a direct access, and on the other hand an outer perception and an outer action, thus an indirect access. With the direct access the consciousness sees and acts directly: body perception and body movement. With the indirect access the consciousness sees and acts only indirectly: seeing with the eyes and moving an object with the help of the hands.

These two possibilities are also found in the model of the tube system: if a tube bumps against another tube, this is an external, indirect perception – if one moves within the tube to another place of the tube system, this is an internal, direct perception. The same is true for actions.

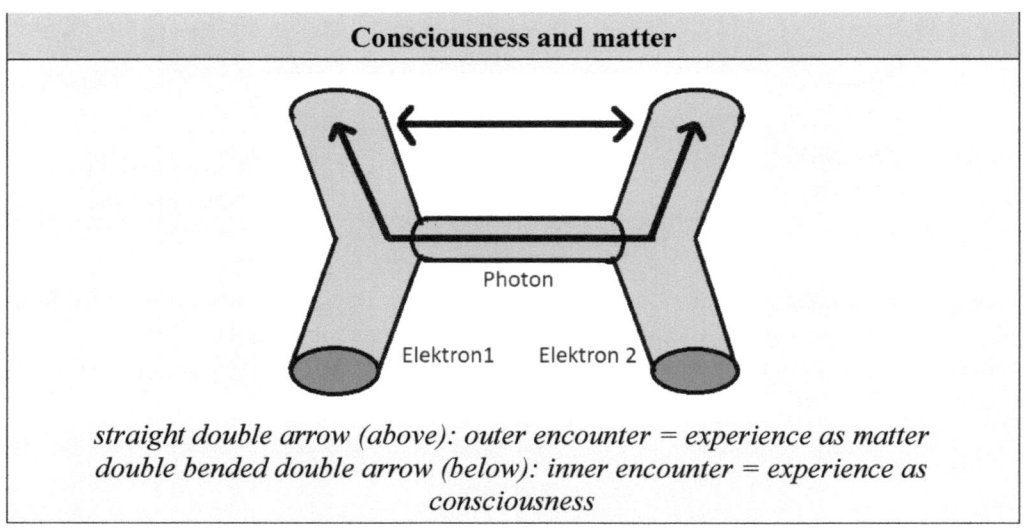

Consciousness and matter

straight double arrow (above): outer encounter = experience as matter
double bended double arrow (below): inner encounter = experience as
consciousness

Consequently, in this tube system model, one can experience everything as matter by experiencing the world from the outside (straight double arrow); and one can also experience everything as consciousness by going inside the tube system to another part of the world (double-bent arrow).

These two possibilities will probably become a little more illustrative with an example: One can touch one's left hand with the help of one's right index finger and perceive it through the right index finger – this is the external, indirect perception through which one experiences the left hand as matter. However, one can also go inwardly with one's consciousness into one's left hand and perceive it directly from within – through this one experiences the left hand as consciousness.

II 4. d) Expansion of Consciousness

If this model is any good, it should also be possible to find in it the conspicuous thresholds of consciousness whose existence has become clear in the earlier considerations.

Why is it relatively easy for the consciousness to perceive things in the own body and to act with the own body? And why is it in contrast somewhat more complex to extend the own consciousness with the help of telepathy perceptively to other things or to move other things with the help of telekinesis?

First of all it is obvious that the parts of the human body are much more closely connected with each other than e.g. the body with the earth. More connections should also mean easier accessibility for the consciousness.

Furthermore, the connection between the body and the earth consists only of gravitation – within the body, however, there is a multitude of electromagnetic connections by which, for example, the atoms in the molecules and also the molecules in the cells are held together.

Of course, there are also quite simply the electromagnetic stimulus lines of the nerve pathways.

In physics, there are three basic types of forces and thus of interactions: the very weak gravitational force, the moderately strong electromagnetic force, and the very strong color force, that is limited to the interior of atomic nuclei.

Interestingly, the five domains of the Kabbalistic Tree of Life, when applied to physics, are characterized in a symmetrical way by these three forces. These five areas are represented by the Middle Pillar[3]:

---

3   It would be rather laborious to describe these theme in detail – it would be necessary to analys the whole structure of the Tree of Life. A complete description of the connection between the fundamental forces and the Tree of Life may be found in my book „Blüten des Lebensbaumes II“.

Kether	- God	- gravitation
Da'ath	- deity	- electromagnetic force
Tiphareth	- soul	- color force
Yesod	- psyche	- electromagnetic force
Malkuth	- body	- gravitation

It would seem, then, that the range of consciousness is determined by the nature of the interaction by which consciousness is connected with something else:

- It is easy to perceive something inside the body and to act there (electromagnetic force).

The electromagnetic force is also the force that acts in the neural pathways that coordinate the perception and the movements. If one does not want to understand the consciousness simply as a side effect of these electromagnetic currents in the brain, nevertheless the question remains about the transition from the nerves to the consciousness.

- It is a little more difficult to grasp in the body also areas which are less strongly connected by the electromagnetic force like e.g. the bones, the hair, the fingernails, the blood, the content of the kidneys, the bladder, the intestine etc. (gravitation, mechanical cohesion).

- It requires an even greater effort to become aware of one's own soul (color power).

The expansion of the consciousness becomes apparently always difficult there, where there are no intensive connections preferably of the electromagnetic kind.

However, the experiments with telepathy show that every human being is able to perceive something telepathically without any preliminary training if the experimental set-up is suitable.

An easy experiment: Person A puts a postcard/photo each in about 20 envelopes. Person B, C, D and E sit around a table and concentrate for three minutes on one of these envelopes that lies on the table. Then they write down what they saw. Afterwards they compare their notes and construct out of those motivs, that occur more then just once in their notes a picture – the foundation of this „telepathic scetch" are those motivs that have been seen by three or four persons. Now you open the envelope and compare the telepathic description with the real picture – it works always. Ideally this experiment is done with a larger group of persons – for example a class in school. It's rather convincing, if you have eight or nine successful groups at once.

From this it follows that it cannot be difficult in principle to perceive something telepathically – it is only necessary to try it out, to proceed in a reasonable way and then to practice the process in order to become more familiar with it.

The telepathy experiment shows that the thresholds of consciousness are not a fundamental obstacle, but only the transition to another realm – and one only needs some knowledge and experience to extend one's waking consciousness to these other realms.

It feels clearly different to perceive something with the eyes or to perceive something telepathically. The feeling in telepathy is more like remembering.

II 4. e)   Time in the Tube Model

The tubes in this model run along the time – the circular super-strings become tubes only if one considers their movements through the time.

If one now wants to change with his consciousness into another person or an object, there are plenty of such tubes to everything: All things affect each other with the help of gravitation.

Since energy quanta including the graviton fly with speed of light, all people and things on the earth would be attainable in clearly less than one second – telepathy needs thus at least on the earth as well as no time for the "information transmission".

It would be interesting to see if getting information about things at greater distances, such as the Earth-Pluto distance, takes the time it takes light (and also a graviton) to get from Earth to Pluto and back – which is about 12 hours. Unfortunately, an experimental setup, with which one could check this, is probably hardly feasible – unfortunately …

One could conclude from this model that it should be possible for consciousness to travel into the past and into the future – after all, the tubes all run along the time axis as well.

Therefore, in the Feynman diagrams and in the tube diagrams based on them, there are no exactly horizontal, i.e. "timeless" lines or tubes, because in these diagrams the perpendicular is the time axis and time passes with every process. However, since the energy quanta (gravitons, photons, gluons) fly with light speed, they need only tiny fractions of a second for their paths. Therefore, the slant of these energy quantum lines (which shows the elapsed time) is so small that one can leave them out – even if there are no really horizontal lines in these Feynman diagrams.

One can travel with the consciousness so fast in the tube system (just with the speed of light) that one can perceive all things on the earth telepathically almost immediately, thus in the present. According to the tube model telepathy moves very probably with the speed of light, because it corresponds to a movement inside the energy quantum tubes.

These considerations of the time in the tube diagram, which point among other things to the possibility of "consciousness time travels", are at the moment only a conclusion from the model.

However, one can verify these conclusions and thereby confirm the correctness of the model – but this will be done in a later chapter.

II 4. f)   The Usefulness of a Model

The tube system model is of course only a model, but at least it offers the possibility to describe the consciousness/matter duality, the consciousness thresholds and the consciousness extensions (telepathy, telekinesis) with a very simple picture.

Moreover, this model has been derived from today's physical theories and physical methods of representation – so the physical side of this model corresponds completely to the models and graphs used in today's physics.

My friend Jörg Wichmann once said, *"Nothing is more practical than a good theory."*

B Structures and Dynamics

The previous considerations were mainly concerned with the relationship between consciousness and matter – simply because magic means, among other things, that physical effects can be triggered by consciousness. Moreover, the consciousness/matter duality is one of the greatest mysteries in our world.

Next, in this chapter, the differences and equalities of consciousness and matter will now be examined and described in more detail. This will also make the transitional area between the two clearer.

III Analogy and Mathematics

The most important tool of physics is mathematics. The most important tool of magic is analogy.

These two tools are different – and also the point of view, under which they regard the world, is different. Therefore also the results of these two points of view should be different – even if the same world is regarded.

From this it follows, among other things, that one cannot explain magic with physics and likewise that one cannot explain physics with magic. But one can combine both views to a more complete picture, since they both describe the same world.

III 1. Quantity and Quality

The most important tool of physics and the natural sciences in general is mathematics. It compares quantities, that is, quantities of the same things.

The most important tool of magic and also of astrology and all other oracles and omens is analogy. By it qualities are compared.

Since magic stands between the completely free consciousness (inside) and the completely determined matter (outside), magic should be creative, thus have access at the same time to the freedom as well as to the impressed forms of the outer world.

To this it fits well that magic deals with qualities and not with determined quantities or with the completely unstructured and therefore free unity.

The qualities of magic contain both freedom and determination. These two things combined together yield creativity.

III 2.   Quantity-equality and Quality-equality

Mathematics as the most important scientific tool considers quantity-equalities. Equations like "2+2=4" mean that there are equal quantities to the left and right of the equal sign. The symbol "=" indicates, like a scale, that there is the same quantity to the left and to the right of this sign.

It also means that there are the same units to the left and right of the "=". The equation "2apples + 2apples = 4apples" is correct; the equation "2apples + 2pears = 4apples", on the other hand, is incorrect; the equation "2apples + 2pears = 4fruits", on the other hand, is again correct. So in a mathematical equation, quantities are compared within the same thing – that thing is the quality of what is counted in that equation.

In a mathematical equation only one quality like "apples" is considered – but mostly these are only very general qualities like the weight or the length or the duration.

Of course there are also more complex equations like "$2m \cdot 2m = 4m^2$" or "force = mass $\cdot$ acceleration", so e.g. "$8N = 2kg \cdot 4m/sec^2$". In this kind of equation, the quality "N" (Newton) on the left side of the equation has been decomposed into "$kg \cdot m/sec^2$" on the right side. Nevertheless, there are forces on both sides – the force has only been broken down into the components that make it up on the right side of the equation.

This principle "in every equation there is the same unit/quality on the left side and on the right side" is also valid for very complex equations or for equations which show rather unexpected relations like e.g. "$E = m \cdot c^2$".

Mathematical equations thus always consider only one quality – but they describe precisely the quantity relations within this one quality.

The analogies used in magic and astrology describe qualities, but not quantities. For example, in astrology the following things correspond to Mars: in the body the muscles, in the psyche the aggression, in the objects the weapons, in the professions the soldier, in the state the military, in the chemical elements the iron and so on.

By analogies the element with the same quality can be found in different fields. It is also possible to represent this connection like an equation: "muscles ① weapons".

In contrast to mathematics, where on the left side and on the right side of the "=" are equal quantities, on the left side and on the right side of the analogy sign "①" are equal qualities.

Since these "magic equations" refer in each case to a certain quality, one can furthermore attach the quality in this analogy to the "Ⅺ" symbol. This looks then as follows: "muscles Ⅺ^{Mars} weapons".

This analogy equation can of course be even more complex and include several things: "muscles Ⅺ^{Mars} weapons Ⅺ^{Mars} iron Ⅺ^{Mars} warrior".

So it is obvious that both in natural sciences and in magic, equations are used to describe the world: In the natural sciences these are quantity equations – in magic these are quality equations.

III 3.   The View of Analogy

Analogies have a great variety and many different possible applications.

III 3. a)   The Analogy Grid

The analogy mostly uses a grid of qualities to determine in which place, in which "compartment", in which "drawer" in such a grid the thing under consideration belongs. Some of these grids can also be called "matrix" or "mandala".

Some of such quality systems are:

- the 2 primordial opposites Yin and Yang (China),
- the 2 primordial opposites fire and ice (Germanic),
- the 2 primordial opposites water and earth (Mesopotamia, Egypt),
- the 2 primordial opposites Sulphur and Mercurius (Alchemy),
- the 4 elements (= fire, water, air, earth),
- the 5 elements (= 4 elements plus the quintessence),
- the 5 Chinese elements (= fire, water, wood, metal, earth)
- the 7 main chakras,
- the 8 trigrams (I Ching),
- the 10 planets,
- the 12 signs of the zodiac,
- the 40 elements of the Kabbalistic Tree of Life,
- the 64 hexagrams of the I Ching,
- the 78 Tarot cards,
- the 256 domains of the West African Ifa Oracle,
  etc.

Such systems have the advantage that one can practice to assign all things and events e.g. to one of the four elements or the quintessence. Thus, after a while, one is able to recognize the elemental affiliation and thus the quality of a thing quite quickly.

All these systems are complete pictures of the world – they represent the world as a complete group of qualities.

One can distinguish three types of analogy grids:

- One can think of these kinds of grids as a complete matrix. Some of them are also ordered like a matrix, i.e. they can be represented as a square grid in

44

which all things in the same column or in the same row have a common quality. Thus, the 64 hexagrams of the I Ching form a square of $8 \cdot 8 = 64$ squares. The Ifa oracle, on the other hand, forms a square of $16 \cdot 16 = 256$ squares.

- Others of these grids are mandalas. Thus, the four elements form the four sides of a square or circle, in the center of which is the quintessence. In the zodiac, the twelve zodiac qualities form a circle, in the center of which is the sun, i.e. the quality of the center. In both cases, the center (quintessence, sun) is also a symbol of consciousness and of the soul, that is, of the next higher level and, therefore, of the origin of the diversity of entities in the outer area of the mandala.

- The third group of grids represents development sequences. This group includes the Tree of Life, the Planetary Sequence, the Tarot Cards, the Chakras, and also the Zodiac, which is both a part of a mandala and a developmental sequence.

Besides these analogy systems, however, there is also the possibility of comparing two systems without the aid of a grid.

For example, if you compare a horse-drawn carriage with a car, there are, among others, the following analogies, i.e. the qualitative and therefore also functional correspondences:

- Carriage   ⦿ Car
- Coachman   ⦿ Driver
- Reins   ⦿ Steering wheel/gas pedal/brake
- Horse   ⦿ Engine
- Horseshoe   ⦿ Tire
- Fodder   ⦿ Gasoline
    etc.

III 3. a)   The "Analogy Effect" or "The Law of Analogy"

In magic it can be observed that "like acts on like" or that "like develops like". This is the correspondence in magic to the causality in physics.

- In astrology there is an analogy between the position of the planets at the time of birth and the character of the person born at that time.

- In homeopathy, a disease is cured with a remedy that produces in a healthy person the symptoms from which the sick person suffers.

- In an oracle such as the tarot cards, the whole system represents a complete image of the world and is therefore analogous to the world. If one draws a card as an answer to a certain question, one receives (via the „law of analogy") the card, that shows the quality that is the answer to the question.

- In magic, with the help of will and imagination, and possibly also through a ritual, a symbol is emphasized that represents ons's goal. The symbol is, so to speak, the analogy essence, i.e. the desired quality. For example, those who want to become rich use the symbols corresponding to Jupiter (" Ⅱ^{Jupiter}") or to the King of Coins (" Ⅱ$^{King\ of\ Coins}$") from the Tarot.
The emphasis on this symbol then invokes the desired thing through the analogy (" Ⅱ").

III 3. c)   The Quantum Entanglement

Probably the so-called "quantum entanglement" from physics is an example of an analogy effect in physics. The term "quantum entanglement" means that two quanta are coupled in their behavior and behave symmetrically, although there is no direct effect between them. The two quanta under consideration maintain a symmetry that does not need a causal exchange of any information or effect between these two quanta.

III 3. d)   Mythology

In the mythological worldview, analogies are the basic ordering principle. By these analogies the variety of the world becomes clear. One of the most important analogy complexes in the mythology of almost all peoples is based on the course of the sun:

The Analogy Complex of the Four Seasons					
Season	spring	summer	autumn	winter	spring
Time of day	morning	noon	evening	night	morning
Point of the compass	east	south	west	north	east
Grain	sowing	growth	harvest	store	sowing
Man	birth	life	death	beyond	rebirth

From such basic analogies arose, among other things, the idea of the combined grain-god and god of the dead, who dies every autumn at harvest and is reborn every spring when the grain sprouts: The life of man and the life of grain are analogies.

This god is also the archetype of reincarnation – of course the origin of this image explains only the image used, but says nothing about whether reincarnation actually exists or not.

III 3. e) Rightness

In the natural sciences the knowledge of phyical structures and connections is aimed at, which then make it possible to cause desired effects. For example, mechanics is one of the bases for the construction of machines. The desired quality is "functioning".

In all magical-mythological worldviews, there is a corresponding central quality that can best be translated as "rightness," but which also contains the aspects of safety, security, rhythm, and beauty.

This rightness arises when one acts in the right way in the right place. This ranges from the right sowing date to the careful making of an arrow to the knowledge about one's own power animal or horoscope.

The direct access to this correctness is one's own soul, which one can find in the "inner conversation". The Sumerians most vividly described the meaning of this rightness, which they called "Me" ("Mother-Quality"): *"Without one's own Me one succeeds in nothing – with one's own Me one succeeds in everything."* The Sumerians looked for this "Me" both in their own inner being (soul) and in the outer being (mother-goddess).

The Sumerians called this quality "Me" (mother), the Egyptians called it "Ma'at" (mother), the Germans "Sidr" (ancient way), the Celts "Fhirinne" (truth), the Romans

47

"Ritus" (wheel), the Slavs "Pravda" (truth), the Hittites "Aya" (wheel), the Indians "Rita" (wheel) or "Dharma" (poetic meter), the Persians "Asha" (wheel), the Greeks "Dikaios" (justice), the Chinese "Tao" (way), the Tibetans "Tashi" (happiness), the Navahos "Hozhong" (beauty), and so on.

This term can be found in just about any magical-mythological worldview, as it is the central concept in a worldview dominated by analogies.

There is sometimes also a term for the "non-rightness", which is e.g. with the Egyptians "Isfet" and with the Hopis "Koyaanisqatsi".

In natural sciences this rightness is the mathematical correctness, thus the agreement of the quantities on the left side and on the right side of the "=" sign.

In magic and mythology, rightness is the matching analogy, that is, the matching of the qualities to the left side and on the right side of the "①" sign.

> C. G. Jung once said, *"The principle of causality states that the connenction of cause and effekt is inevitable. The principle of synchronicity states that events are connected by synchronicity and meaning."*

III 4.   Causality and Simultaneity

Natural sciences consider causalities, i.e. cause-effect relationships in time. This results in a picture that is completely oriented to the time line and to quantities.

Magic, on the other hand, considers analogies, i.e. simultaneities of states and events. From it a picture results, which rests completely in the moment and orients itself to qualities.

From this difference follows that natural sciences and magic look at the world from completely different directions and consequently also receive two completely different observation results.

From this difference follows furthermore that one cannot explain magic with natural sciences and just as little one can explain natural sciences with magic. Natural sciences and magic examine the world from different points of view, look at different aspects of the world and also carry out different experiments.

However, since natural sciences and magic look at and describe the same world, the observational results of natural sciences and magic should be able to be combined to form a more comprehensive view of the world.

Natural sciences look with the one eye – magic looks with the other eye. It would be nevertheless gratifying to see the world once in such a way, as it looks, if one has opened both eyes …

III 4. a)   Physical Quantities from the Point of View of Magic

Physical quantities like volume, weight, temperature, kind of substance etc. are given in quantity and kind like "4km", "32°C" or "3 liters of water".

From the point of view of magic the indications "km", "°C" and "water" are clearly more interesting than the numbers which stand before these indications. "Water" can be clearly assigned to the quality of the element "water", with the temperatures ("°C") there is probably a connection to the element fire, while "km" can hardly be classified – perhaps there is a connection to the element earth.

The number in front of the designation indicates, how much there is of the designated. In magic, this corresponds approximately to the degree of concentration on the signified.

III 4. b)   Magical Connections from the Point of View of Physics

Magical parameters are given as qualities: "a sword on the altar as a symbol of Mars" or "reciting the Buddhist Heart Sutra three times" or "calculating and interpreting the horoscope of the person concerned".

In all three cases, a quality is precisely described: Mars, heart chakra/Buddha, and horoscope/self-knowledge. This corresponds to the designations behind the numbers of the physical indications like "3km" or "1kg iron".

A precise quantity specification as with the physical quantities one looks for in vain with the magic specifications – however it is said e.g. that one should consecrate the sword to Mars, recite the heart Sutra with full concentration and interpret the horoskop as vividly as possible.

This intensity demanded here by the consecration, the concentration and the vividness corresponds to the numbers before the physical quantities. However, these "magic quantities" cannot be expressed precisely by numbers, but only by the level of intensity that must be reached for the intention to be effective.

III 4. c)   Comparison

As the two preceding considerations show, both natural sciences and magic use "measure and number". However, while the natural sciences always measure and compare the precise quantities of a single quality, magic considers a precise quality and its intensity.

The intensity is, so to speak, the "quantity of consciousness" directed to the symbol, that is, to the analogy. This intensity is responsible for the effectiveness of magic.

In magic, both the right analogy (quality) and sufficient intensity are needed:

- A precise choice of analogy results in a precise quality, but if the intensity is "0", nothing happens.

- A high intensity with a very imprecise analogy, on the other hand, has either no effect or an undesirable effect.

So both natural sciences and magic use "measure and number" – but in very different ways.

The most obvious difference between the two approaches is with respect to time: Natural science considers the temporal development of a process – magic considers the simultaneity of events.

This difference can be represented as a diagram in which the vertical axis is time and the horizontal axis is present and place. Physics considers all things along the time axis in their temporal development – magic considers all things across this axis as analogy in a particular moment.

Time in Physics and in Magic

physics considers the vertical axis: changes in the flow of time
magic considers the horizontal axis: analogies in the present time

Within this diagram, physics could be called the "vertical worldview" and magic the "horizontal worldview".

IV Comparison: Forms in Physics and Magic

Since physics and magic describe the same world, both ways of looking at things should be able to be combined into a unified world view.

However, the question arises how to find the points where the two worldviews can be related to each other in a meaningful way: In the magic worldview there are no precise quantities and in the physical worldview there are no analogies ...

However, what is the same in both worldviews are the structures and dynamics that become visible when looking at the world. The smallest units of structures are simply the angles between two things. However, there are also quite a few clearly more complex structures which can be found both in physics and in magic.

Thus, one can develop the unified worldview a good deal further by looking at the structures that are common to both worldviews. These structures seem to be (figuratively spoken) something like "God's sketches", according to which he has designed the world ... Natural sciences and also magic can grasp only a section of this "divine construction plan" because of their one-sided ways of looking at it. The part of this "blueprint", which one can see from both ways of looking at it, must be a very central, fundamental part of this blueprint.

The comparison of the coinciding structures in physics and magic could therefore bring to light interesting insights into the world.

IV 1. Structure: The Angles

The simplest of all structures is the angle. The angles have the same qualities in physics as they have in magic, astrology, stone healing etc.

IV 1. a) The Angle of 0°

This angle means that two things are together, are adjacent to each other, are attracted to each other, are connected to each other.

A 360° step is necessary to get back to the starting point.

Physics: In the physical world the gravitation which pulls all things to each other corresponds to this angle. This force is so to speak "one-polar", since there are no different forms or alignments of the gravity: Everything attracts everything.

The form created by gravity is the sphere: suns, planets and moons.

The two electrons in the innermost electron shell of an atomic nucleus, i.e. in the so-called "s-orbital", have the shape of a sphere.

Magic: In astrology, the conjunction is the 0° angle: two planets enter into a "marriage" and always appear and act together.

Quality: This angle embodies identity, cohesion and integration.

IV 1. b) The Angle of 180°

At an angle of 180° two things face each other – they are "two-polar".
It takes two 180° steps to get back to the starting point.

Physics: The two-polar force in the world is the electromagnetic force. It has the two electric charges "+" and "–" and the two magnetic poles "north" and "south". They appear as magnetic fields, which emerge e.g. at the poles of galaxies, suns and planets and form there bundled rays, which extend far into the universe (e.g. at the north pole and the south pole of the earth) – these are called „jets".

One can also regard the expanding big bang impulse and the contracting gravitation as such a polarity.

The second innermost electron shell of the atoms, i.e. the "p-orbital", has the shape of two spheres facing each other as seen from the atomic nucleus.

A very simple example of a 180° angle is the swing that swings back and forth between two poles.

Magic: In astrology, the opposition is the 180° angle. Through this aspect, two planets are joined together as complementary opposites.

The signs of the zodiac that oppose each other in the zodiac also form complementary opposites: the "I" of Aries and the "you" of Libra, the taking in of Taurus and the taking out of Scorpio, the curiosity of Gemini and the purposefulness of Sagittarius, the "inside" of Cancer and the "outside" of Capricorn, the particular of Leo and the general of Aquarius, and the detail of Virgo and the vastness of Pisces.

The "I Ching" oracle is based on the consideration of the transformation possibilities of the yin/yang basic opposition in the world. Very similar pairs of complementary opposites in mythology are Fire and Ice (Germanic), Earth and Water (Mesopotamian), Earth God and Sky Goddess (Egyptian), Sulphur and Mercurius (Alchemy), etc.

Also the inner man and the inner woman as well as the principle of the two sexes in general belong to these basic polarities.

The I Ching has a binary structure, i.e. there are two basic qualities: Yin and Yang. The same basic principle is also found in the West African Ifa Oracle.

This order goes back to the number system of the people in the Paleolithic Age, of which many remains can be found in the early cultures. In this system, counting was done in the simplest possible way: There were only the numbers "1", "2", "4" and "8". With them one could designate all quantities up to 15 precisely and in an easy way – and larger precise numbers were not needed at that time. For example, a "7" was a "4+2+1" and an "11" was an "8+2+1".

In today's decimal system, a more complicated but also more effective way of denoting quantities is used. For example, a "147" is a complex calculation: "$1 \cdot 100 + 4 \cdot 10 + 7 \cdot 1$".

By combining the two original qualities Yin and Yang to "Yin-Yin, Yin-Yang, Yang-Yin and Yang-Yang" the four simple qualities were created. By a further combination of these four bigrams with Yin and Yang the eight trigrams result. Finally, by combining two trigrams each, the 64 hexagrams are created. These hexagrams are then arranged on an $8 \cdot 8$ square grid (this is also the origin of the chess board and the checkers board).

In the Ifa Oracle, one has gone one step further and developed 256 qualities, which are arranged on a $16 \cdot 16$ square grid.

These two oracles illustrate the quality of "2", which becomes more and more differentiated by doubling: $2 \cdot 2 \cdot 2 \cdot 2 \cdot 2 \cdot 2 = 256$.

Quality: The 180°-angle has the character of a complementary counter-set.

IV 1. c)   The Angle of 120°

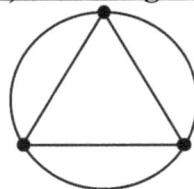

In an equilateral triangle there are three interior angles of 120°. This angle is therefore "triangular" or "three-polar".

It takes three 120° steps to get back to the starting point.

Physics: In physics there is a three-polar force in the atomic nuclei and in the protons and neutrons, which is called "color force". In gravitation there is only one polarity; in electromagnetic force there are two poles ("+" and "−") which together give the neutral "0"; in color force there are three poles ("red", "yellow", "blue") which together give the neutral "0" ("white"). This color force represents a very great cohesion – it is the strongest of all forces.

Magic: The astrological 120° aspect is called "trine" ("triangle"). It represents a "friendship", that is, a firm cohesion between two planets.

In the zodiac, the three signs of the zodiac with the same element (fire, water, air or earth) form a triangle.

In stone healing, minerals with a trigonal (triangular) crystal lattice promote simplicity, constancy, rhythm, tranquility, enjoyment, peacefulness, natural clarity, tolerance, balance and friendships – which corresponds exactly to the quality of the astrological trine.

Quality: The 120° angle creates steady, solid connections.

The three basic forces			
	gravitation	*electromagnetic force*	*color force*
energy quantum	graviton	photon	gluon
Angle	0° (360°:1=360°=0°)	180° (360°:2=180°)	120° (360°:3=120°)
Polarity	one-polar	bipolar	three-polar
Shape	point	complementary opposition	triangle
astrological aspect	conjunction	opposition	trine
Range	infinite	infinite	$2,5 \cdot 10^{-15}$m
relative strength	1	10^{37}	10^{39}
Graph			

IV 1. d)   The Angle of 90°

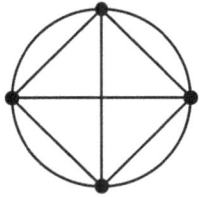

Four angles of 90° make a square in a circle. This angle therefore has an "angular" character.

Four 90° steps are necessary to get back to the starting point.

<u>Physics</u>: The best known "square" in physics is probably the "structure" of light, i.e. the electromagnetic wave (photon). In this wave, the magnetic wave is always at a 90° angle to the electric wave. Both waves oscillate around the same axis, i.e. around the flight direction of the photon. The energy of the photon is alternately in the electric and in the magnetic wave. The energy is successively in the following positions: up (electric), right (magnetic), down (electric), left (magnetic), up (electric), right (magnetic), and so on. Consequently, the change of energy between the electric and the magnetic phase is a circle: up – right – down – left – up – right etc. The superposition of the straight flight direction of the photon with the circular change of its energy between the electric and the magnetic wave results in a spiral motion.

The d-orbitals in the electron shell of an atom form a square or a "cross", i.e. the axes of the two electron pairs are at right angles to each other.

The four cardinal directions are at right angles to each other as seen from the "here". They are the basic orientation in space.

The Cartesian coordinate system consists of two axes intersecting at right angles or, if it is a spatial system, three such axes.

<u>Magic</u>: The astrological square aspect is like a tent pole: it holds two things apart, creating space and freedom.

In the zodiac, the three signs of the zodiac with the same dynamics (cardinal, fixed or mutable) form a square.

The cubic crystal lattice consists exclusively of right angles, which is why the crystals themselves are cubic, i.e. cube-shaped. They promote order, overview, structure, solidity, security, causality, control, firmness, regulation and overview. This corresponds to the character of the astrological square, since this creates space through its width and separation, orders and gives rise to the desire for openness, sincerity and directness – as it was sometimes said in former times: "right-angled to body and soul".

<u>Quality</u>: The 90° angle (square) has throughout the "bulky" character of stretching a space.

IV 1. e)   The Angle of 60°

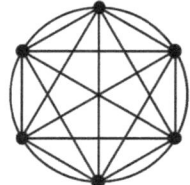

This angle is created when many elements of the same kind are gathered together – it is the angle of group formation.

It takes six 60° steps to get back to the starting point.

<u>Physics</u>: On the same orbit around a planet can circle altogether six moons, if they all have a distance of 60° seen from the planet. Almost every planet has some "mini-moons" called "Trojans" in front of and behind it at a distance of 60° on its orbit.

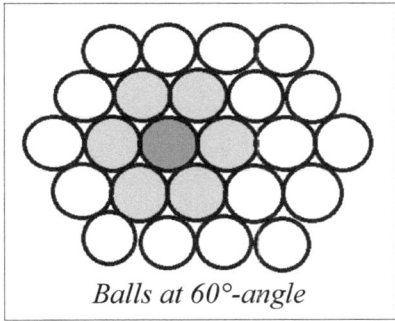

Balls at 60°-angle

If you put balls of the same size (marbles or similar) in a bucket, they will lie at 60° angles to each other.

Since protons and neutrons are also spheres and have moreover almost the same size, they form 60° angles to each other in the atomic nuclei and also in the neutron stars.

The principle of the connection of a large number of equal elements to a structure by the 60°-angle is also found in the structure of large molecules of carbon or of silicon. These two types of atoms have four free electrons (their "contact arms" for bonding with other molecules) and can therefore combine to form very complex molecules.

In doing so, they often form "rings" that are actually regular hexagons: Carbon forms the familiar benzene ring and hexagonal crystallizing graphite, and silicon forms the phyllosilicates and framework silicates better known as "quartz" or "rock crystal".

These "rings" of carbon or silicon have the shape of a honeycomb. The difference between a quartz and a rock crystal is that in a quartz each layer forms a large molecule and in a rock crystal the entire crystal is a single molecule. So in a rock crystal all the atoms are connected to each other by pairs of electrons that are at 60°

59

angles.

60°-ring molecules			
Carbon		*Silicon*	
Benzene ring C_6H_6	*Graphite* C_n	*Quartz* SiO_2 *phyllosilicates*	*Rock crystal* SiO_2 *framework silicates*

The 60°-structure principle can also be found within the atomic shells of the atoms. Exactly eight electrons fit on the second innermost orbital of an atom. These eight electrons are divided into a "vertical" pair of electrons (p-orbital) and a "horizontal" circle of six electrons (f-orbital), which are arranged honeycomb-like in 60°-angles.

The structure of snowflakes by 60° angles is generally known:

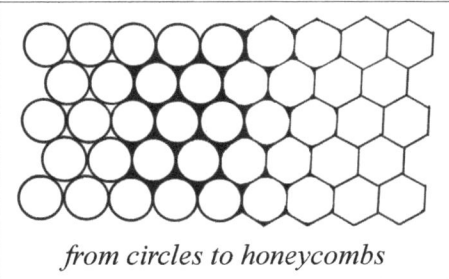

from circles to honeycombs

The merged circles (spheres) form honeycombs by merging, thinning and straightening the edges. The internal angles of the honeycombs are 60°.

If one looks for the shortest connection between four points arranged in a square, one will assume that this shortest connection is reached by the three side lines of the square. On closer inspection you will probably notice that the two crossing diagonals are still a bit shorter than the total length of three side lines. However, this is still not the shortest possible connection, because this is based on the honeycomb pattern characterized by the 60° angle and looks as follows:

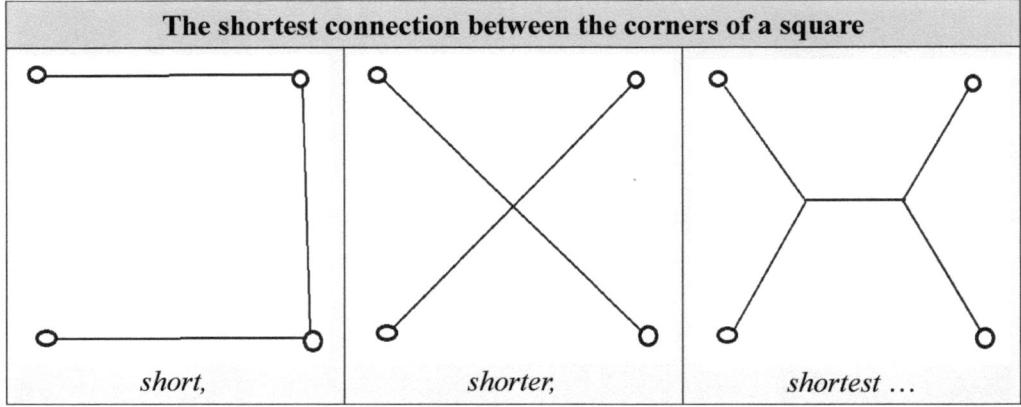

The shortest connection between the corners of a square

short,   *shorter,*   *shortest ...*

<u>Magic</u>: In astrology, the sextile joins two planets into a group that can work together, but does not have to. The sextile is the social aspect.

Six consecutive sextiles join in the zodiac in the form of a honeycomb either the three fire signs with the three air signs or the three water signs with the three earth signs. In this way, the active fire/air group and the passive water/earth group are formed.

"flower of life"

In magic, the 60° rosette is sometimes used for harmonizations. This chart is often called the "flower of life".

The minerals with a hexagonal cristal grid promote efficiency, purposefulness, consistency, straightforwardness, sincerity, clarity, analytical thinking, agility in strategy and tactics, and critical faculties. This is more about execution than direction: craftsmen, but not managers. This corresponds to the astrological sextile aspect.

<u>Quality</u>: The 60° angle forms harmonic groups of the same or very similar elements.

IV 1. f) The Angle of 30°

The 30° angle is found in a very central place in physics: in the superstring. Twelve 30°-steps are necessary to get back to the starting point.

Physics: Today's physics describes all particles and energy quanta as superstrings. A superstring looks (very simplified) like a circular vibrating string. The smallest superstring is divided into twelve zones, which are alternately a wave crest and a wave trough. Viewed from the center of the superstring, these twelve circular sections are each 30° large.

 The principle of progression that characterizes the astrological 30° aspect is found in physics as heat, in chemistry as a catalyst, and in biology as an enzyme: the element that stimulates transformation. However, no concrete 30° angles are recognizable here.

 Magic: The 30° semisextile is in astrology the aspect that stimulates further development of a state to the next state, which results logically from the first state.

 Moreover, the basis of astrology, i.e. the zodiac itself, is also divided into twelve equal sections of 30°, precisely into the twelve signs of the zodiac.

 From their function also teachers, gurus, therapists and the like would belong to the "people with semisextile quality". However, here also is the concrete 30°-angle missing.

Quality: The 30° angle indicates transformation and further development.

IV 1. g)   The Angle of 150°

This angle is known from astrology (where it is very prominent), but otherwise it seems to play no role.

It takes twelve 150° steps to get back to the starting point. The 150° aspect is the only one of the angles considered here that has to pass through the whole circle several times to get back to its starting point. Like the 30° angle, it touches all twelve points. One can therefore already conclude from this geometrical peculiarity that the 150° angle it is similar to the 30° angle, but at the same time it will be clearly more unsteady.

Physics: According to the quality of this angle in astrology one could assume that the 150° angle plays a role in the constant transformation of neutrons into protons and vice versa in the atomic nucleus.

Possibly also the weak interaction belongs to this angle quality, since this is effective with transformations in the atomic nucleus (decay processes).

These transformations would fit well to the fact that the 150°-aspect touches already purely geometrically all twelve possible points in the circle and makes thereby very restless jumps.

Magic: In astrology, the quincunx, i.e. the 150° aspect, represents the constant tidying, ordering, cleaning, tensioning, nourishing, nurturing, and so on.

Quality: The 150° angle probably has the quality of constant transformation and rearrangement.

The Quality of the Angles		
Angle	***Quality***	
	Natural Sciences	*Magic, Mythology etc.*
0°	**Identity and Cohesion**	
	- gravitation - s-Orbitals	- astrology: conjunction - identity
30°	**Stimulation and Evolution**	
	- the sections of the twelve-divided superstring circle - physics: heat, igniting spark - chemistry: catalyst - biology: enzyme	- astrology: semisextile
60°	**Grouping of Equal Elements**	
	- most space-saving arrangement of equal elements - many equal and closely arranged spheres in one area - many equal and closely arranged spheres in space (atomic nucleus, neutron star) - honeycomb - snowflakes - carbon molecules (benzene ring) - silicon molecules (quartz) - several moons in the same orbit - f-orbitals - 60° rosette („flower of life") - shortest connection between the corners of a square	- astrology: sextile - hexagonal crystal lattice

The quality of angles		
Angle	**Quality**	
	Natural Sciences	*Magic, Mythology etc.*
90°	Spanning a Room	
	- cardinal points - coordinate system - electromagnetic wave - d-orbitals	- astrology: square - cubic crystal lattice - symbolism of the cardinal points
120°	Solid, Inseparable Cohesion	
	- color power	- astrology: trigon - trigonal crystal lattice
150°	Constant Transformation	
	- weak interaction	- astrology: quincunx
180°	Complementary Opposition	
	- electromagnetic force (+ / −) - big bang momentum and gravity - p-orbitals	- astrology: opposition - pair of primordial deities - two primordial elements (Yin and Yang, Sulphur and Mercurius, Fire and Ice etc.)

IV 2.   Structure: The Twelve-divided Circle

The essence of "12" has already been briefly considered, but it is also worth taking a closer look, since this number describes a very basic structure in the world.

If you search for twelve-part systems, you can find all kinds of things. However, it makes sense to take a closer look at what you have found.

IV 2. a)   The Zodiac

The actual existence of the zodiac can be verified at any time by calculating a horoscope. So this zodiac is something that can be found in the world.

Of course, it is not known for sure whether the Mesopotamian duodecimal system, which is based on the "12" and not on the "10" like our decimal system today, was formulated on the basis of the zodiac or whether the duodecimal system came first and then simply fit the zodiac. Probably the duodecimal system came first, for in the beginning there were also 10-part and 11-part zodiacs.

IV 2. b)   The Mythological Groups of Twelve

After the discovery of the zodiac, the "12" became a symbol of completeness and thus a symbol of the round and whole. Therefore it was obvious to form groups of twelve wherever one wanted to characterize a group as complete and thus also as perfect: the twelve petals of the heart chakra, the twelve gods on Olympus, the twelve Aesir in Asgard, the twelve apostles, the twelve knights of the Arthurian round, etc.

IV 2. c) The Color Circle

Some circles of twelve look quite convincing at first, but turn out to be rather arbitrary on closer inspection. One of them is the color circle.

The three basic colors are red, yellow and blue – you can represent them as a triangle. By mixing two colors each, you get orange (yellow/red), violet (red/blue) and green (blue/yellow) – you can represent them as a hexagon (honeycomb). If you now mix the colors next to each other again, you get a twelve-part circle: red – red-orange – orange – golden-yellow – yellow – may-green – green – turquoise – blue – blue-violet – violet – red-violet – red.

However, this circle of twelve has three flaws:

1. In it are missing all the browns, which are created by mixing all three primary colors.

2. In it are missing the colors "white" and "black".

3. The three basic colors are based on the fact that we humans have three receptors in our eyes, which can perceive three different wavelengths of the light. However, the number of these receptors is quite different in other creatures – there are insects which have sixteen different light receptors and which, among other things, can also perceive UV light and the polarization of light, both of which are completely invisible to us.

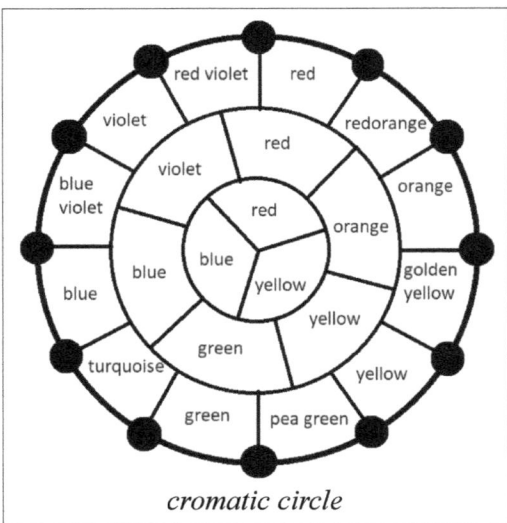

cromatic circle

Thus, the color wheel has twelve parts, but it is not a fundamental, but a random structure of twelve.

This can already be seen in the graphics, if one illustrates the mixture of the twelve colors mentioned – the convincing symmetry is missing …

IV 2. d)   The Cranial Nerves

From the human brain twice twelve nerve tracts go into the body to different areas (one group of twelve into the left half of the body, one into the right half of the body). However, since no convincing assignment to the twelve signs of the zodiac can be found, the twelve number seems to be coincidence at this point.

Unfortunately, I have not been able to find out whether this division into twelve is only present in humans or in general in all animals with a more complex nervous system. If the twelve cranial nerves should be a general structure, it would be presumably nevertheless a fundamental structure, which is based on the character of the "12". Then a more thorough investigation of the relationship between the cranial nerves and the zodiac would be necessary.

In this investigation it might be helpful to begin with the simplest examples of twelve cranial nerves, since in the course of evolution sometimes correlations and symmetries which had been clearly discernible at the beginning have changed, losing their symmetry to some extent.[4]

IV 2. e)   The Acupuncture Meridians

There are points on the body in Chinese medicine that are used in acupuncture, acupressure, massage, meditation, etc., to produce certain effects in the body.

These acupuncture points are located on lines called "meridians". Like the cranial nerves, they occur in two equal groups of twelve lines each on the body. Most of them can be quite easily and clearly assigned to the signs of the zodiac.

Since these meridians are well researched and, like the cranial nerves, occur in a group of 2·12, i.e. as 12 pairs, the probability increases that the number "12" of the cranial nerves in humans is not just a coincidence after all.

IV 2. f)   The Organ Clock

The Chinese organ clock assigns the organs to one twelfth of the day – each organ is therefore particularly active for 2 hours. This organ sequence corresponds for the most part to the zodiac. The organ clock thus seems to be a fundamental order, even if it cannot yet be completely assigned to the zodiac.

---

4   I've desribed these connections and evolutions in my book „Chakren und Organe".

IV 2. g)   The Clock

The 24 hours of the day, i.e. the 12 day-hours and the 12 night-hours are obviously not a fundamental order, but simply a grid created on the basis of the duodecimal system.

IV 2. h)   Superstring and Zodiac

The zodiac is the fundamental structure of astrology. If the world should be really constructed according to the principle "inside = outside", the twelve-part circle should also be found in a central place in physics. This twelve-part circle in physics is the "Heisenberg spin chain", which is called today mostly briefly "superstring".

The superstring is the mathematical description of all elementary particles and all energy quanta in our world – thus it is the basic structure of everything that exists.

The actual "substance" of the world is from the point of view of today's physics the space-time. All energy quanta and elementary particles are curvatures of the space-time, so to say small "mountains" and "valleys" in the space-time. There is ultimately only the one, all-encompassing space-time – one can understand it as the physical correspondence to God.

Superstrings are the simplest form in which space can curve into a "delineated, distinguishable entity."

Such a superstring can be thought of as a very, very tiny circular string that vibrates up and down in twelve places, making it a twelve-part standing wave.

The standing wave is one of the very few physical phenomena that consists of a group of equally sized but sharply defined areas – and is thus an equivalent to the zodiac with its twelve equally sized and sharply defined signs of the zodiac.

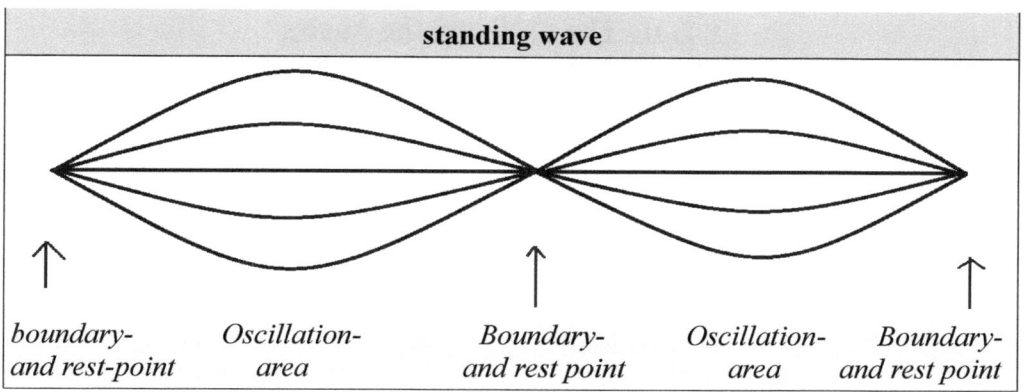

standing wave

| *boundary- and rest-point* | *Oscillation- area* | *Boundary- and rest point* | *Oscillation- area* | *Boundary- and rest point* |

Both the zodiac and the superstrings have the structure of a circular, twelve-part standing wave:

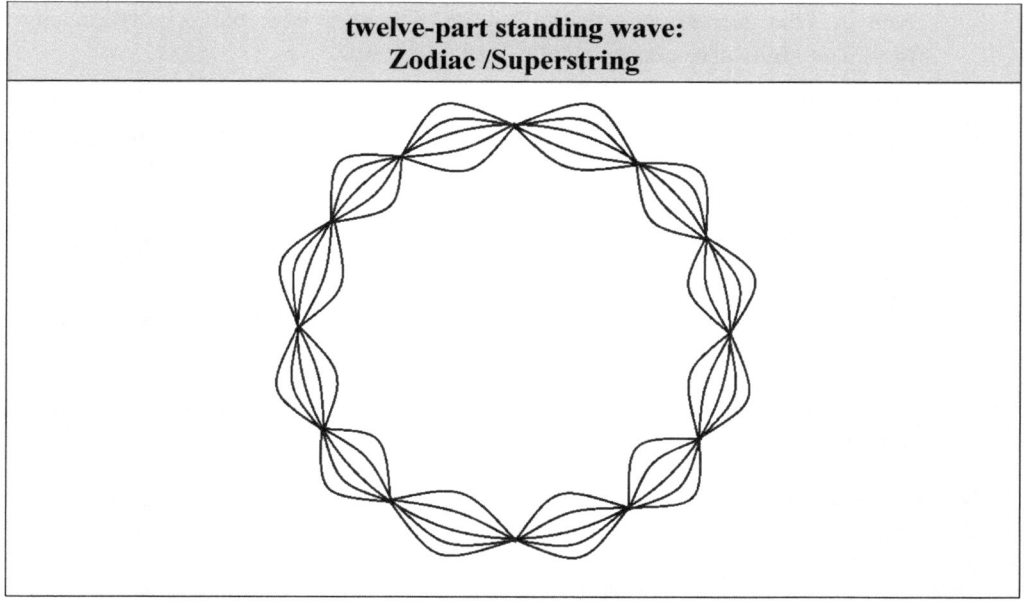

twelve-part standing wave:
Zodiac /Superstring

Each wave crest corresponds to a zodiacal sign. The unmoved zero points are the boundaries between the zodiacal signs.

IV 2. i) The "12" and the Angles

The quality of the angles in physics corresponds to the quality of the aspects in astrology. The astrological aspects are in turn closely related to the zodiac. One can virtually derive the zodiac from the aspects or vice versa.

In the zodiac, each sign is identical with itself. This corresponds to the **0°** aspect of the conjunction.

Each sign is the opposition complement to the sign opposite to it. This corresponds to the **180°**-aspect of the opposition. The "planetary rulers" of these two signs are also opposites: There are the three opposition-complement pairs "Moon/Sun – Saturn", "Mercury – Jupiter" and "Venus – Mars".

Each sign is a "friend" of the two signs that are **120°** away from it. These three signs have the same element (e.g. fire). This corresponds to the trine. These three signs also form a triangle geometrically.

Each sign has a separation ("tent pole") to the two signs standing **90°** away from it. This corresponds to the square. Together with the opposition sign, these four signs also geometrically form a square.

Each sign has an "acquaintance" to the two signs standing **60°** away from it. This corresponds to the sextile. Together with the two trine signs and the opposition sign, they form a honeycomb of six sextiles. The elements in this honeycomb are either fire and air or water and earth.

Each sign is the progression of the sign before it and the foundation of the sign after it. This corresponds to the **30°** aspect of the semisextile. The twelve semisextiles together form the developmental dynamics of the zodiac, leading from one sign of the zodiac to the next in the course of the year.

Each sign is in constant conflict with the two signs that are **150°** away from it. This corresponds to the quincunx aspect.

Each sign of the zodiac defines in six different ways (aspects) all other eleven signs of the zodiac – this is a 132-fold definition. A higher form of interdependence and integration is hardly imaginable …

One can also assign the aspects directly to the zodiacal signs – both have the same basic qualities.

Here one can distinguish the directions of orientation "inside" and "outside". "Inside" is the orientation towards what you want for yourself; "outside" is the orientation towards what you want in the world.

Aries: the "here and now" of the conjunction

Taurus: the gathering of what is pleasant by the inwardly oriented semisextile

Gemini: the playing with what is there of the inwardly oriented sextile

Cancer: the protection of the inside by the inward oriented square

Leo: the alignment with the center by the inward trine

Virgo: the ordering by the inward oriented quincunx

Libra: the harmonizing and unifying complementary opposition

Scorpio: the tension of the outwardly oriented quincunx

Sagittarius: the aspiration of the ideal through the outwardly oriented trigon

Capricorn: the securing of the outside by the outwardly oriented square

Aquarius: the formation of community by the outwardly oriented sextile.

Pisces: the being carried by the whole by the outwardly oriented semisextile

In astrology there is a second system of twelve: the twelve houses. The houses are oriented to the time of day, whereas the zodiac is oriented to the season. Both systems coincide in their qualities.

One can describe each sign of the zodiac in a differentiated way by combining the signs of the zodiac and the houses:

For example, a Virgo behaves in the 1st house like a Virgo: ordering, healing, paying attention to trifles, etc.

In the 2nd house, on the other hand, she behaves like a Libra: striving for harmonious order. So in the 2nd house is the sign that follows Virgo, that is, the next sign in the zodiac sequence as seen from Virgo.

In the 3rd house she behaves like a scorpion – she checks carefully who or what she gets involved with to avoid any disturbance of her order. In the 3rd house is the sign after next, looking from Virgo.

In the 4th house she behaves like a Sagittarius – she lets only the best into

73

her living room, into her circle of friends. In the 4th house is the 4th sign, if you count from Virgo onwards.

etc.

Of course, in the horoscope of a person with Virgo ascendant there sometimes can be Scorpio or Capricorn in the 4th house, that is, a sign before or after Sagittarius. This is not about a specific horoscope, but about the inner logic of the zodiac.

Thus, in relation to the themes of the 2nd house (personal hygiene, possessions, clothing, house, earning money, etc.), each sign behaves like the sign that follows it in the zodiac:

Scorpios are demanding on 2nd house themes like Sagittarians.

Sagittarians are realistic like Capricorns in 2nd house themes.

The Capricorns are systematic-skilled like Aquarians in 2nd house themes.

The Aquarians are trusting on 2nd house issues like Pisces.

etc.

Both the inner logic of the zodiac and the relationship between the zodiac and the aspects is even much more detailed than has been presented here.[5]

So we can say that the qualities of the astrological aspects and therefore also of the physical angles are derived from the zodiac – and presumably also from the inner structure of the superstring.

In this connection a question arises because there is an inconsistency here:

The three basic forces have different polarity: gravity is one-polar, the electromagnetic force is two-polar ("+" and "–" or north and south) and the color force is three-polar (red, yellow and blue).

From the combination of these three polarities the twelve-structure of the superstring and also of the zodiac should actually result. This combination of polarities is mathematically seen a multiplication. However, one receives only the "6" as result: "$1 \cdot 2 \cdot 3 = 6$".

One can imagine this also geometrically: If you start from a point (1) and combine it with its opposite pole (2), you get 2 points. If one combines these two points with the 3, you have to add to each of these two points the two points 120° left and right of them – thus one receives altogether 6 points. However, the zodiac is not 6-divided,

5   A more complete description of these connections and symmetries may be found in my book „Astrologie".

but 12-divided.

By the three basic forces one receives a 6-structure, which reminds of the two 6-groups of zodiac signs, which are connected by 6 sextiles to a honeycomb: the 6 fire/air signs and the 6 water/earth signs. The six signs in one of these two groups are connected by conjunctions, sextiles, trines and oppositions – they contain the 1-polar aspect (conjunction), the 2-polar aspect (opposition), and the 3-polar aspect (trine).

These two groups are connected in the zodiac by semisextiles (advancement), squares (separation) and quincunxes (transformation) – these aspects are not to be found inside one of these two groups of six signs. These three qualities apparently describe the element that makes two groups of 6 become a group of 12.

Among the basic forces there is a fourth force whose status within the basic forces is not so clear: the weak interaction. It causes that a neutron can change into a proton and an electron or that a proton can change into a neutron and a positron (positively charged electron). These two decay processes would quite fit the properties of semi-sextile, square and quincunx.

From the combination of the polarities of the three basic forces a "6" results. To let it become a "12", one would have to multiply it by "2". But "2" is already the polarity of the electromagnetic force. So a basic force is searched, which is not the electro-magnetic force, but has the properties of the electromagnetic force – it is probably an "offshoot" of the electromagnetic force.

Since the exchange particles (energy quanta) of the weak interaction have an electric charge, it is obviously the force searched for here, which lets the "6" become the "12".

Does the weak interaction have the polarity "2" or "4"?

If its polarity would be "2", the "$1 \cdot 2 \cdot 3 = 6$" would become a "$1 \cdot 2 \cdot 3 \cdot 2 = 12$".

But the polarity "2" already belongs to the electromagnetic force and there-fore cannot also be the polarity of the weak interaction.

If its polarity would be "4", the "$1 \cdot 2 \cdot 3 = 6$" would become a "$1 \cdot 2 \cdot 3 \cdot 4 = 24$".

However, one can also imagine that the "2" and the "4" overlap to a "4", which would result in a "12" again: "$1 \cdot 3 \cdot 4 = 12$". The "2" would then be con-tained in the "4".

Such multiple definitions exist also in the zodiac, where each zodiac sign is connected by altogether eleven aspects with the other eleven zodiac signs and is defined in this way.

However, there is no clear 4-polarity of the weak interaction recognizable by direct physical observation.

IV 2. j) Mandalas

Mandalas are often used in religion, magic and spirituality. They are graphics in the form of overviews, grids, maps, etc., which arrange the totality of the elements of a system in a meaningful way.

A simple mandala is, for example, the arrangement of the four elements in the four directions of heaven on a circle with the quintessence (light) in the center. Such mandalas can be quite complex and contain several concentric circles and also more than just 4 directions. In the center is the origin, the essence and the goal, towards which the rest of the mandala represents the path.

In such a mandala the whole world can be placed. In the simple example of the mandala of the four elements and the quintessence, all things are assigned to one of the four elements. A mandala is consequently a systematic picture of the world, which reduces the world to a few characteristics.

This need for overview, completeness and order exists of course also among physicists.

A well known example of a "physical mandala" is the periodic table of the chemical elements. In it, all existing chemical elements are arranged in an order that makes sense in several respects: It shows the increasing number of protons, neutrons and electrons of the elements, the increasing weight of the elements, their outer electrons and thus their affiliation to a certain chemical reaction mode, their radioactivity, etc. By its structure, however, the periodic table of the elements is a special form of a matrix and not a mandala.

Another "physical mandala" is the so-called SO3-symmetry, which (simplified) shows how which particles can change into which other particles.

A very interesting "physical mandala" are the four elementary particles of which the complete matter is built: the up-quark, the down-quark, the electron and the neutrino. They correspond to the four elements (fire, water, air, earth) in the astrological zodiac.

These four basic particles occur in three sizes, which obviously correspond to the three dynamics in the zodiac (cardinal, fixed, mutable).

What could now be criteria for an assignment of these particles to the four elements?

The two quarks are clearly heavier than the other two particles. Therefore they could correspond to the two heavy elements water and earth.

The up quark has the charge "+2/3"; the down quark, on the other hand, has only half the charge "-1/3". So the up-quark is stronger and should correspond to the water, which is still a little more agitated than the earth.

The electron has with "-1" the biggest charge and should therefore correspond to the fire.

The neutrino has no electric charge and also otherwise hardly an effect and could correspond to the air.

From these considerations the assignment results, which is shown in the following table.

It is to be noted, however, that although the four elementary particles certainly correspond to the four elements and that just as certainly the three sizes of the elementary particles correspond to the three astrological dynamics, the assignment of the four elements to the four elementary particles is based only on conjectures. Therefore, behind the element assignments in the table there is a "?" in each case.

Since a few years the "Higgs-Boson" has been added to the elementary particles, but it belongs to another category of particles. It gives the elementary particles their mass and is therefore something similar to the electric charge of a particle.

The 12 basic elementary particles			
	1. family *normal particles* *creating zodiac signs*	*2nd family* *heavy particles* *formative zodiac signs*	*3. family* *very heavy particles* *mutable zodiac signs*
leptons with charge -1	electron	muon	tauon
Fire (?)	Aries	Leo	Sagittarius
Quarks with charge +2/3	"up" quark	"charm" quark	"truth" quark
water (?)	Cancer	Scorpio	Pisces
Quarks with charge -1/3	"down" quark	"strange" quark	"beauty" quark
Earth (?)	Capricorn	Taurus	Virgo
Neutrinos with charge 0	Electron-neutrino	Muon-neutrino	Tauon-neutrino
Air (?)	Libra	Aquarius	Gemini

IV 2. k) Birth and the "12"

The places where the "12" can be found are quite interesting and make the nature of the "12" even more clear.

The zodiac is found where a person is born: The birth chart is calculated on the time of a person's birth. However, such horoscopes can also be calculated for animals, companies, states and the like. All living beings, things and organizations receive their horoscope at the moment of their becoming independent (cutting the umbilical cord, hatching from the egg, signing the founding document etc.). This means that the general astrological quality of the moment "freezes", so to speak, in the moment of becoming independent and shapes the person or thing for a lifetime.

Also superstrings, whose simplest forms have a division into twelve, are born out of space-time, so to speak, and then form "mountains" and "valleys" in the plane of space-time.

The horoscope of a person born on Earth refers to the zodiac. This zodiac is anchored in the earth and not in the stars – it is calculated from the winter and summer solstices and the spring and autumn equinoxes. Since the zodiac is, so to speak, the structure of the "aura" of the Earth, one can wonder if this Earth zodiac was created when the Earth was formed from stardust and small pieces of rock.

Does the sun also have a zodiac or even birth chart? And our entire galaxy? And the world as a whole? Can twelve-part circles be observed everywhere at these places of origin and times of origin? And do these structures of twelve stand in a kind of hierarchy of the form "universe – galaxy – sun – earth – human being" to each other?

We do not know – but the central role of the "12" in our world and therefore also in the unified world view, which is sketched in this book, has already become very clear.

IV 3.   Dynamic: The Three Steps

It is not enough to look whether one finds a "3" somewhere in order to be able to grasp the quality of the "3", because after all there could be quite different three-part structures.

Four such types of three-part structures are:

1. <u>Three elements form a whole.</u> This structure is found, for example, in the astrological trine and the color force.

2. <u>A process in which one thing (1) has an effect (2) on another thing (3).</u> This structure is also found, among others, in the grammar of most languages: subject (1) – verb (2) – object (3).

3. <u>An opposition which causes a development.</u> This is the well-known principle of "thesis – antithesis – synthesis".

4. <u>The three steps of a development.</u> These three steps could be called "foundation, elaboration and utilization". They can be found, for example, in astrology as "cardinal, fixed, mutable" or in anthroposophy as threefoldness with the three elements respectively phases "Lucifer, Arhiman, Christ".

In this chapter, the 4th possibility of a three-part structure just mentioned will be considered in more detail.

This structure is very widespread and will be described here only on the basis of some important or well known examples.

IV 3. a)   Three Steps

The three steps could also be called "flow dynamics":

1. A stream flows.
2. It flows into a pond and forms two eddies to the left and right of the point of the water mouth.
3. The water of the stream mixes with the water of the pond.

One can also summarize this dynamic in a more general way:

1. impulse
2. encounter with the environment to it
3. exchange with the environment

One can also rewrite these three steps more generally:

1. expansion
2. delimitation
3. contact

IV 3. b) Astrology

In astrology these three steps are found in the three dynamics:

1. cardinal
2. fixed
3. mutable

The four cardinal signs are the four creative signs that create something new:

Aries (cardinal fire = spontaneous action)
Cancer (cardinal water = sensitive feelings)
Libra (cardinal air = new contacts)
Capricorn (cardinal earth = new foundations)

The four fixed signs are the signs that take, represent and develop their own point of view:

Leo (fixed fire = egocentricity)
Scorpio (fixed water = the intensity of one's own feelings)
Aquarius (fixed air = the universal utopia)
Taurus (fixed earth = enjoyment)

The four mutable signs are the signs that live in a variety of actions:

Sagittarius (mobile fire = idealism)
Pisces (mobile water = trust)
Gemini (mobile air = curiosity)
Virgo (movable earth = skill)

IV 3. c)   Elementary Particles

In elementary particles, these three steps occur as the three forms in which the four basic elementary particles up-quark, down-quark, electron and neutrino occur.

IV 3. d)   The Sun

The sun shines because in the high pressure in its center hydrogen atoms are melted together to helium atoms whereby a lot of energy (photons) is released. This pressure is caused by the large mass of the sun.

During this nuclear fusion a lot of energy is released, which heats up the matter in the center of the sun. This heated matter is lighter than the "cooler" matter on the outside of the sun and therefore rises to the surface of the sun, spreads out there, cools down and then sinks back down to the center of the sun. This convection current is something like a "liquid volcano."

Since the hot sun radiates both light ("heat") and matter particles, it also imprints its surrounding space. This imprinting develops three layers, which surround the sun like three hollow spheres lying into each other with the sun as their centre.

1. The photons, ions and other particles, which are ejected from the sun into the space, are called "solar wind".

Space is not simply empty, but filled with atoms and tiny pieces of rock called "stardust."

The particles of the solar wind collide with this stardust and push it away from the sun – the solar wind blows the dust away from the sun and out into space.

Since the solar wind is about equally strong in all directions and the stardust is about equally dense everywhere around the sun, an approximately spherical region has formed around the sun in which the solar wind has swept all the stardust outward. This is the solar wind region that has been completely shaped by the sun.

2. If one sweeps dust, a heap of dust forms before the broom, since the dust does not dissolve by the sweeping into nothing, but only is pushed away. The solar wind has meanwhile pushed the complete stardust, which was around the sun, to beyond the orbit of Pluto. There is now a hollow sphere of stardust and of the particles which the sun has emitted.

This layer is called "shock front", because at it the solar wind collides with the stardust – both the "new" stardust at this place in space and the "old" stardust, which the solar wind has pushed away outward in front of it.

This layer is of course still an almost completely transparent collection of dust, but here the dust is denser than further out in space. The mass of this shock front is about the same as the mass of the earth.

3. The shock front is not static, but is pushed out by the solar wind constantly further into the universe. Thereby the shock front collides with the stardust beyond the shock front, whereby this new stardust is pushed away from the shock front. This can be imagined like the wave in front of a moving ship, why this area is also called "bow wave".

These three spherical areas around the sun have clearly distinguishable properties:

- The area of the <u>solar wind</u> is completely shaped by the nature of the sun – it is, so to speak, the area of the uninhibited self-expression of the sun.

- The area of the <u>shock front</u> arises from the encounter of this self-expression with the environment – thereby boundaries and forms are created.

- The <u>bow wave</u> finally sends impulses into the surrounding space and perceives the surrounding space – here a contact to the surrounding space can be found.

Self-expression, form and contact are the three steps that are clearly shown here. They obviously correspond to the three astrological dynamics cardinal (creating), fixed (shaping) and mutable (manifold).

There is another element in the space around the sun, which will be of importance in the further considerations: the two jets of the sun.

galaxy with two jets

In galaxies, suns and planets there are ions, i.e. electric charges. If an electric charge moves, a magnetic field is created. If this movement is a rotation around its own axis, the magnetic field is bundled to two jets, which exit along the rotation axis, i.e. at the two poles. These two radiating magnetic fields are called "jets". They reach out into space by a multiple of the diameter of the rotating sphere (galaxy, sun, planet). Even black holes have two jets emerging at the poles of their rotation axis.

As magnetic fields they also accelerate ions, which then can be seen like a shell around these jets and finally form a diffuse cloud in space far away from the celestial body from which they originate. In particular, the clouds at the end of the jets of galaxies can be huge – they are so large and dense that they can be photographed with the help of telescopes.

These jets and the clouds at their ends look like the swirl-like shapes a stream forms when it flows into a pond.

The jet pairs also resemble the p-orbital of two electrons: two spheres facing each other, forming a "dumbbell".

IV 3. e)   The Chakras

The chakra system is quite similar in structure to the surrounding space of the sun. In the center is the heart chakra – it is the center of the entire chakra system. In it lies the identity of the person: It is the "temple of the soul". The heart chakra corresponds to the sun – it is the "sun chakra".

From the heart chakra, a ray called "sushumna" protrudes downward and upward, which can be understood as a life force channel. It corresponds to the two jets of the sun – the heart chakra also rotates like the sun ("chakra" means "wheel").

Around it there are three hollow sphere-shaped areas, which correspond exactly in character to the three areas around the sun. They each form a chakra where the sushumna crosses them.

84

1. innermost hollow sphere: unhindered self-expression (⊙ solar wind)
   a) below: Solar Plexus – unhindered physical self-expression
   b) above: Throat Chakra – unhindered social self-expression

2. middle hollow sphere: demarcation (⊙ shock front)
   a) below: Hara – inner hold
   b) above: Third Eye – outer orientation

3. outer hollow sphere: contact (⊙ bow wave)
   a) below: Root Chakra – physical contact
   b) above: Crown Chakra: spiritual contact

The chakra system is build the same way as the sun's surrounding space: Both have the same structure.

The chakras are also linked to the states of consciousness: The heart chakra with deep sleep, the solar plexus and throat chakra with dreaming (sub-consciousness), the hara and third eye with waking, and the root chakra and crown chakra with ecstasy.[6]

The Symmetry of the Chakras				Symmetry			
Chakra	*Quality*		*Consciousness*				
crown chakra	social contact	understanding	ecstasy				
third eye	social structure	orientation	waking				
throat chakra	social impulse	to show oneself	dream				
heart chakra	identity	soul	deep sleep				
solar plexus	physical impulse	action	dream				
hara	physical structure	inner support	waking				
root chakra	physical contact	touch	ecstasy				

---

6 A detailed description of the chakras and their properties and functions may be found in my book „Das Chakrensystem mit den Nebenchakren".

This three-step can be found in the chakra system a second time:

     1. the actual <u>chakra</u> inside the body at the sushumna,

     2. the <u>Kshetram</u>, which is the mirror image of this chakra in the front and back of the body surface, and

     3. the <u>point on the aura</u> about an arm's length in front of and behind the body, respectively, where one makes contact with other people and things.

IV 3. f) Comparison: Solar Surrounding Area and Chakras

The similarity of these two systems can probably be most clearly illustrated by two graphs:

Sun-space and chakra system

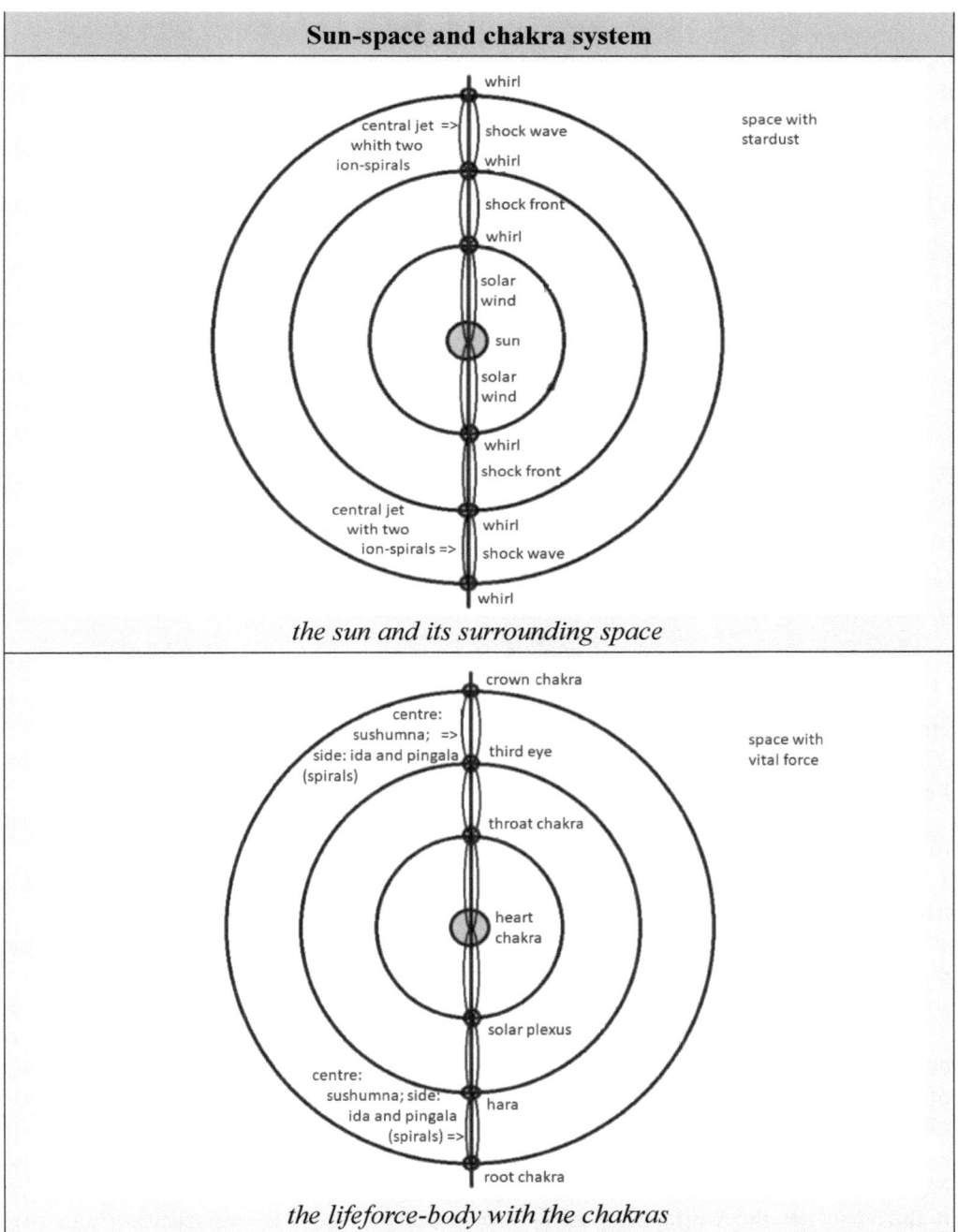

the sun and its surrounding space

the lifeforce-body with the chakras

IV 3. g) The Vajra

The Vajra is an Indian symbol that evolved from the Neolithic lightning symbol in Mesopotamia.

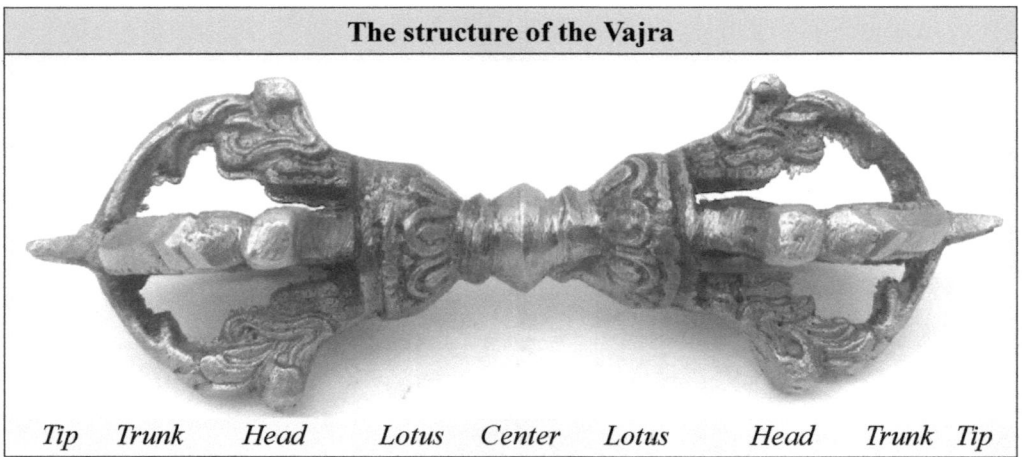

The structure of the Vajra

Tip   Trunk   Head   Lotus   Center   Lotus   Head   Trunk   Tip

It has a spherical center that expands symmetrically in opposite directions (Ⓤ sun and heart chakra).

The first expansion are the two lotus flowers (Ⓤ solar wind space and solar plexus/throat chakra).

The newly emerging form are the four elephant heads that emerge out of each lotus (Ⓤ shock front and hara/third eye).

The perception of the world is represented by the meeting of the four elephant trunks on the very outside (Ⓤ bow wave and root chakra/crown chakra).

The two rods in the middle of each of the four elephant heads represent the bipolar expansion (Ⓤ jets and sushumna).

Originally, the vajra was a symbol of lightning among the Indo-Europeans and among the Neolithic peoples in Mesopotamia. It is also known from the magic wands of the Germanic seers, from the Greeks, the Hittites, the Sumerians and the Babylonians.

One cannot conclude from this symbol and its long history that people in the Neolithic Age already knew the chakra system or even the solar wind, but it seems as if the idea that the world originated from a unity ("Tao") by polarization into two opposites ("Yin and Yang"), and likewise that things develop in three steps from a center (among other things also the eight "trigrams" of the I Ching), is already very old.

From the analogy between the chakra system and the solar system two important conclusions arise:

- In the center of the sun's circumference is the sun, so in the center of the chakra system there must also be a "sun" – that is the soul.
  The sun is the cause of the threefold structured environment of the sun (solar wind, shock front, bow wave) – without the sun this structure would not exist at all. So, by analogy, the soul in the heart chakra must also be the cause of the two groups of three chakras above and below it.

- The solar system and also the chakra system are by their structure an expansion from a center, which leads in three steps to a concretization.

Since the chakra system is the basic structure of the psyche and thus of the consciousness of man, it follows from this dynamic of radiation, expansion and self-expression that this very expansion dynamic is also the basic dynamic of the soul.

The exact analogy of this expansion in consciousness (psyche) and in matter (sun) shows once again quite clearly that consciousness and matter contain the same structures – as was to be expected.

IV 3. h) The Fountain

The dynamics of the three phases can probably be most simply and vividly illustrated by means of a fountain:

1. the rising jet
   ① solar wind
   ① solar plexus and throat chakra
   ① cardinal signs

2. the unfolding fountain
   ① shock front
   ① hara and third eye
   ① fixed signs

3. the falling drops
 - ⓘ bow wave
 - ⓘ root chakra and crown chakra
 - ⓘ mutable signs

IV 3. i)   The "Volcanoes" of the Sun

As already described, hot matter rises from the center of the sun, spreads out on its surface and then sinks cooled down again into the depth.

This dynamic corresponds exactly to the fountain with its rising jet, its spreading fountain and its falling drops.

This kind of dynamics is called "convection current".

IV 3. j)   The Continental Drift

Convection currents also exist in the Earth, but they are much weaker and slower than in the Sun.

The largest upwelling site for hot matter from the Earth's interior is currently located in the middle of the Atlantic Ocean and extends from Greenland down to Antarctica: the "mid-Atlantic ridge". The matter rising from the earth's interior causes a long mountain chain to form there on the sea floor, which has been pushing Africa/Europe on one side and America on the other apart for 200 million years by its upward bulging and by its spreading. This rising lava is the cause of the whole continental drift on the earth.

Here we find again the three dynamics:

- The "rising" is the rising hot lava that forms volcanic mountains.

- The "unfolding" is the horizontal movement of the continents (continental drift).

- The "falling down" is the so-called subduction zones, where two continental plates push over each other, causing the lower one to sink into the depths of the earth. One such place is off the west coast of America, for example, where the American plate is pushing over the Pacific plate (because America is being pushed westward into the Pacific by rising lava in the Atlantic Ocean). This creates the mountains on the American west coast (Rocky

90

Mountains, Andes) and the ocean trenches off this coast: the continental plate is lifted as it is pushed up and the Pacific plate is pushed down.

On a small scale, this process is also found in a volcano:

- Lava rising inside the volcano
- lava fountain above the volcano (the "volcano-mountain")
- lava flowing down the volcano

IV 3. k) The Gulf Stream

This three-part dynamic is also found in the world's oceans: For example, the Gulf Stream is heated in the Gulf of Mexico (rising water) and then flows northeastward on the ocean surface past Europe to the Arctic (spreading water), where it cools again (sinking water) and flows back into the Gulf of Mexico at the depth of the ocean.

IV 3. l) The Wind

Convection currents also exist in the atmosphere. However, because air is much more mobile than magma in the sun, lava in the earth, and also much more mobile than water in the ocean, air moves much faster along these flow paths. Over hot places like the Sahara, the air heated there rises (ascending) and in cold places like the Arctic, the air cooled there falls down again (descending). The horizontal flow of the air masses to the place where they rise or fall is the wind (spreading).

IV 3. m) The Soup Pot

The same process can be observed on a small scale when cooking soup: In the pot some places are formed where the soup bubbles up (rising), while at the edge of these places the soup sinks back down to the bottom of the pot (falling). In the process, the herbs and the like floating on top are pushed aside by the bubbling waters as in a small continental drift (spreading).

IV 3. n) The Tree of Life

The Kabbalistic Tree of Life is basically a very simple structure:

- Its basic principle is unity as the starting point and multiplicity as the result, and in between a developmental step or differentiation of unity to multiplicity.

- The middle step of this "three-step" (the developmental step) is differentiated once again into three steps – this creates the five areas on the Tree of Life, also called the "Middle Pillar". They are separated from each other by the four transitions.

- Finally, these three middle steps are then subdivided once again into three steps each. In this way a differentiated, eleven-part development structure results.

The derivation of the Kabbalistic Tree of Life I					
Derivation			*Sephiroth* (areas)	*Planets* (Assignment)	*Tree of Life* (graphic)
I	*II*	*III*			
1.	1.	1.	Kether	Pluto	
2.	2.	2.	Chokmah	Neptune	
		3.	Binah	Uranus	
		D	Da'ath	Saturn	
	3.	4.	Chesed	Jupiter	
		5.	Geburah	Mars	
		6.	Tiphareth	Sun	
	4.	7.	Netzach	Venus	
		8.	Hod	Mercury	
		9.	Yesod	Moon	
3.	5.	10.	Malkuth	Earth	

Since understanding this derivation of the Tree of Life graphic is fundamental to understanding the Tree of Life, here is another graphic representation of this derivation:

the derivation of the Kabbalistic Tree of Life II				
1. a system	2. The first differentiation into the three phases "Origin, Development, Goal".	3. the second differentiation of the middle phase into three sub-phases respectively	4. the third differentiation of the three sub-phases into three sub-sub-phases each	5. the traditional representation of these eleven areas as the Tree of Life

Since this structure can be derived in a simple, logical way, it can be found in everything – from the structure of a vacuum cleaner to the classical ballet and from the chakra system to the constitution of a state.[7]

The sequence of the three dynamics "cardinal, fixed, mutable" in astrology or the three areas around the sun are easy to grasp because they are very simple. The Tree of Life, however, is nothing else than these three steps – only that the middle one of these three steps has been divided in it once more into three steps and these three middle steps then once more into three steps each, so that the middle step then consists of three groups of three, thus of nine steps.

The Tree of Life is the most differentiated analogy structure known so far. It consists of 40 elements: the 11 spheres (Sephiroth), the 22 paths between them, the 3

---

7   These applications of the Tree of Life may be found in my book „Blüten des
    Lebensbaumes II".

triangles (2/3/D, 4/5/6, 7/8/9) and the 4 transitions between the five areas on the Middle Pillar.

This structure is found everywhere – even in the "heart of physics", as which one can call the superstring theory a little poetically.

IV 3. o) Examples of Application of the Tree of Life

The following three examples show how a system can be structured with the help of the Tree of Life. Maybe these examples help grasping its inner dynamics and make the Tree of Life a bid more concrete and vivid.

The German State

The basic structure corresponds to the three areas "origin – development – movement" on the tree of life, which is identical with the three astrological dynamics "cardinal – fixed – mutable".

   I.   The basis of the German state is the Basic Law. This is the highest sphere, the original impulse, the "rising".

   II.   This impulse is then differentiated in the middle sphere – the "unfolding".

   III.   through this, finally, the behavior of the people arises as a result – the "falling down", the concretization.

The second of these three stages is then divided into three phases:

   II 1.   From the basic law the general conditions are derived – the creating "rising up".

   II 2.   On the basis of these framework conditions, the government then acts – "unfolding".

   II 3.   The government's instructions are finally implemented by the administration – the "falling down" in the image of the fountain.

These three "sub-phases" of the second phase are each subdivided again into three "sub-sub-phases", which again have the same dynamics:

II 1. Foundation Phase:

II 1. a)   After the foundation of the parties (active, ascending element)

II 1. b)   the parties join together to form the Constituent Assembly and adopt the Basic Law (agreement on the manner of development of political activity)

II 1. c)   and elect the Federal President as the representative of the state (executive function).

II 2. unfolding phase:

II 2. a)   The Legislature passes laws (creating),

II 2. b)   the judiciary supervises the implementation of these laws (unfolding)

II 2. c)   and the executive, i.e. primarily the Federal Chancellor, organises the state according to the specifications of the legislative and judicial branches (implementation).

II 3. implementation phase:

II 3. a)   The ministers concretize the laws and the chancellor's instructions (create).

II 3. b)   The implementation of the laws in everyday life is monitored by the police. The interests of the state are protected externally by the military (unfolding).

II 3. c)   Finally, the administration organizes the framework conditions of everyday life of the people (implementation).

These eleven processes in total are made much clearer by the classic representation as a Tree of Life. To the right is first seen the second level of differentiation and to the far right the first level of differentiation.

the German State				
	basic Law		I Foundation	I Foundation
constitutional assembly		parties	II 1. framework conditions	
	constitution federal president			
Judiciary (judges)		Legislature (Bundestag, Bundesrat)	II 2. government	II selfregulation of the State
	Executive (Chancellor)			
military, police		ministers	II 3. administration	
	lower authorities			
	people		III people	III people

<u>Four machines</u>

In the following Tree of Life, four different "machines" are described at the same time to make clear the analogous structure of these machines. These machines are:

     1. vacuum cleaner,
     2. car,
     3. nuclear power plant, and
     4. computer.

The first four sections are identical for all four machines.
The four machines are always represented in the following Tree of Life in the order given above.

Four machines			
	will to simplify work		will to simplify work
Combination of tools		the tools	planning
	construction plan		
Engine: 1. engine 2. engine 3. fuel rod room 4. data processing		load-bearing construction: 1. supporting structure 2. chassis 3. building 4. housing	inner structure
	"cockpit" (for the human as the steering element): 1. handle 2. driver's seat 3. control room 4. place in front of the PC		
Information transfer: 1. cable 2. cable, mechanics 3. cable, mechanics, sensors 4. connection cable, modem, browser, internet		Orientation/alignment in the world: 1. handle, on/off switch 2. steering wheel, gas pedal, brake 3. control of fuel rods 4. keyboard, mouse, monitor	external structure
	Gearbox, power transmission, power supply: 1. intake manifold, power cable 2. gearbox, connection engine-axle, gasoline tank 3. steam-turbine, generator, uranium 4. cable to monitor and printer, power cable		
	Housing, "point of action": 1. suction attachment 2. wheels 3. power supply to the power grid 4. printer, monitor		casing, "point of action"

Vector mathematics

The last example of the application of the structure of the Tree of Life is vector mathematics. A vector is defined by having a magnitude and a direction – for example, the circling of the moon around the earth is described by a vector, or the flight of a stone thrown into a lake.

The Lorenz transformation describes the motion of a vector in space – it is an essential element in the theory of relativity.

Vector mathematics					
	zero point			origin	
angle		axes		coordinates	theory of relativity = Lorenz-transformation
	base vector				
vector subspace		vector space		vector space	
	vector				
size of vector		direction of vector		vector	
	unit vectors				
	matrix			matrix	

These examples show that the "fountain-dynamics" of "rising, spreading, sinking", which one could also call "creation, unfolding, application", is contained in all things. This three-step-dynamic must therefore belong to the basic elements according to which this world has been constructed.

IV 3. p)   The Superstring Theory

The superstring theory used by physicists today is a very complex theory. To describe it, a mathematical model is needed which uses not only the three space dimensions and the time dimension familiar from everyday life, but seven more space dimensions which, however, become visible only in areas far smaller than an electron – these seven dimensions are "hidden", so to speak. One of these seven additional dimensions has the property that it "envelops" the other ten dimensions, i.e.

summarizes them.

This eleven-dimensional mathematical model corresponds exactly to the Kabbalistic tree of life:

- The topmost of these eleven spheres (Kether) corresponds to the time dimension.

- The three spheres below it (Chokmah, Binah, Da'ath) correspond to the three "normal", endless space dimensions.

- The six following spheres (Chesed, Geburah, Tiphareth, Netzach, Hod, Yesod) correspond to the six "hidden" and limited space-dimensions.

- The lowest sphere (Malkuth) corresponds to the "summarizing" dimension.

Tree of Life and Superstring Theory				
Tree of life		*Tree of Life Graphic*	*Superstring theory*	
Sephiroth	*Assignment*		*Quality*	*Dimension*
Kether	God		eternal	1.
Chokmah	gods		infinite	2.
Binah				3.
Da'ath				4.
Chesed	soul		finite	5.
Geburah				6.
Tiphareth				7.
Netzach	psyche		finite	8.
Hod				9.
Yesod				10.
Malkuth	body		summarizing	11.

In the end it is not surprising that also the superstring theory corresponds so precisely to the tree of life, if the tree of life is a structure which is contained in all things.

It may take some time to get used to the fact that there is such a structure, according to which all things from a cell and a bee colony to meditation and the superstring theory are built.

The same concept of the "omnipresent structure" is also found in the I Ching, in the Tarot, in the Mandala of the four elements and the Quintessence and similar systems. What is special about the Tree of Life is ultimately only the differentiation and mathematical precision of this system.

It is of course not possible within the framework of this book to present the many possible applications, fine structures and dynamics of the Tree of Life.[8]

IV 3. q) Tree of Life and Zodiac

The three dynamics from which the Tree of Life is derived are found in astrology as the three dynamics "cardinal, fixed, and mutable".

On the other hand, the zodiac in the form of horoscopes is also found on the Tree of Life at the transitions:

> - A person's natal chart belongs to the "trench" between the realm of the soul and the psyche, as it is created when a soul incarnates and thereby creates a psyche.

> - The transits to a horoscope, that is, the planetary positions at a certain moment in relation to the birth chart belong to the "threshold" between the psyche and the body, which corresponds to the "here and now" of Malkuth.

> - At the "abyss" are found the twelve elementary particles, among others, which correspond to the zodiac.
> One could also assume here the horoscope of the soul, if it arises as an "demarcated drop" out of the "sea of a deity" by demarcating itself from this deity. This process will very likely never be able to be proven with certainty, but it can be experienced in meditation and on dream journeys.

> - To the "First Cause" belongs finally the emergence of the first superstring after the Big Bang – which is like the zodiac a twelve-divided ring.
> Here one can suppose the "horoscopes of the gods" which can be proved of

---

8   These applications of the Tree of Life may be found in my book „Blüten des Lebensbaumes II".

course still much less than the "horoscopes of the souls" and which are quite hypothetical …

Nevertheless, this consideration shows that the tree of life and the zodiac are closely connected with each other.

In the graphic of the Tree of Life the transitions have been represented as thick, gray crossbars.

Tree of Life and Zodiac			
Sephiroth (areas)	Planet (sssignment)	Transitions (zodiac)	Tree of Life (graphic)
Kether	Pluto		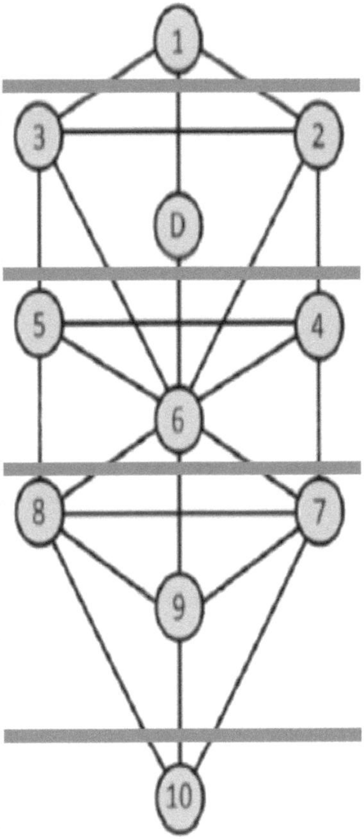
		"First Cause": horo-scope of a deity (?)	
Chokmah	Neptune		
Binah	Uranus		
Da'ath	Saturn		
		"Abyss": horoscope of the Soul (?)	
Chesed	Jupiter		
Geburah	Mars		
Tiphareth	Sun		
		"Trench": horoscope	
Netzach	Venus		
Hod	Mercury		
Yesod	Moon		
		"Threshold": transits (≈ horoscope of a moment)	
Malkuth	Earth		

IV 3. r) Kundalini

The threefold dynamic of the convection flow are also found in the flow of the Kundalini:

1. rising of Kundalini from the root chakra in the center of the body,

2. unfolding of the Kundalini above the crown chakra and

3. flowing down of Kundalini all around the body to the root chakra.

Usually only the life force flow from the root chakra to the crown chakra is called "Kundalini", more rarely the whole life force circuit in the body.

The existence of this circuit allows an interesting conclusion:

- If this life force flow called "Kundalini" were to be triggered from the heart chakra as the center of the chakra system, the life force flow would have to flow from the heart chakra upward and back to the center, and from the heart chakra downward and back to the center (like the blood circuit).

- The life force flow from the root chakra up to the crown chakra and back down again indicates that the life force flows from the earth into the root chakra and then creates this vortex of flow in the person – like a stream flowing into a pond.

- From this it follows that human beings are connected to the earth by a "life force umbilical cord" and are presumably "nourished" by it with life force.

- This "umbilical cord" is an important element in the Kundalini meditations and in awakening the Kundalini.

The rising kundalini as well as the radiance of the life force body that arises from it is depicted in many images and statues of Buddha and Shiva.

the rising kundalini and the radiant aura		

Buddha with Kundalini	*Medicine Buddha with aura*	*Buddha Manjushri with aura*

The Kundalini convection current is also one of the central elements in Yoga, especially in Kundalini Yoga and in its Tibetan version, Tummo.

By concentrating on the lowest chakra, an inner heat is awakened, which then slowly rises in the center of the body, unfolds above the crown, and then flows back down all around the body. The inner heat generated by this meditation also warms the material body during the meditations of the Tibetan lamas in the icy Himalayas.

The rising heat is often depicted as a snake. The unfolding of this heat into a "fountain" above the crown is sometimes represented by seven serpent heads, corresponding to the seven chakras. The descent of the heat around the body is rarely depicted.

IV 3. s) Acupuncture Meridians

The acupuncture meridians run in four groups of three on both halves of the body from the head through the back to the hands, from the head through the chest to the hands, from the head through the back to the feet, and from the head through the chest and abdomen to the feet.

It can be assumed that these twofold symmetrical "4·3=12" meridians correspond to the twelve signs of the zodiac. In the majority of the acupuncture meridians, the relationship to the zodiac signs can also be easily recognized.

Presumably these groups of three meridians also correspond to the three-step, since they correspond to a large extent in a regular way to the signs of the zodiac.

IV 3. t)   The Gods of Time

In mythology, the threefold dynamic is most clearly found among the Indians in the gods trinity Brahma the creator, Vishnu the sustainer (unfolding) and Shiva the destroyer (dissolving).

A similar division into three parts is found in the Indo-Germanic religions in the three goddesses of fate and birth, who are called "Norns" by the Germans, "Parcenes" by the Romans, "Moirs" by the Greeks, and so on. With these three goddesses is connected the image of the spinning of the thread of life (creation), the measuring of the thread of life (unfolding) and the cutting of the thread of life (result).

IV 3. u)   Threefoldness

A special variant of the three-step is the threefoldness, which was formulated by Rudolf Steiner. It corresponds to the "fountain dynamics": the three stages of system development, used mainly in the context of enterprises.

These three stages are:

- 1st stage ("Lucifer"): foundation – a lot of commitment, a lot of work, a lot of movement, new things

- 2nd stage ("Arhiman"): consolidation – rules, determinations, routines, re-assurance, protection

- 3rd phase ("Christ"): Application – rhythm, liveliness, flexibility, cooperation, expansion

IV 3. v)   Summary

The considerations in this somewhat longer chapter show that the three dynamics are an essential element which can be found in many contexts and systems. In the zodiac, for example, they give rise to the twelve signs of the zodiac out of the four elements.

The dynamics of the "3"			
Area	**Dynamics**		
	creating	*unfolding*	*differentiating*
waterspout fountain	jet	fountain ("water-disk" at the upper end of the jet)	drops
sun	rising hot matter	hot matter pouring on the surface	descending cold matter
Earth	rising magma	continental drift and mountain building	sinking continental plates
	rising lava	lava fountain (vulcano-mountain)	descending lava
Gulf Stream	heated water on the sea surface	ocean current	cooled water in the sea depth
Wind	rising air in warm areas	Wind	sinking air in cold areas
Soup pot	rising water	bubbles on the surface	sinking water
Solar wind	solar wind	shock front	bow wave
elementary particle	normal size	increased size	maximum size
Kundalini-Yoga (flow of the vital force)	rising inner heat	unfolding above the crown	descent around the body
chakras	chakra	kshetram	outer image on the aura
Zodiac	cardinal signs: Aries, Cancer, Libra, Capricorn	fixed signs: Leo, Scorpio, Aquarius, Taurus	mutable signs: Sagittarius, Pisces, Gemini, Virgo
Tree of Life	creation	formation	execution
3 gods	Brahma the creator	Vishnu the Sustainer	Shiva the destroyer
3 goddesses of destiny	spinning the thread of life	measuring the thread of life	cutting the thread of life

IV 4. The "4"

In considering the three-step, it has been shown that it is, among other things, an essential element in the structure of the zodiac. Since the twelve signs of the zodiac result from the fact that the four elements appear in these three dynamics, the question arises whether there is not also a fundamental structure formed by the "4" – just as the developmental dynamic of the "3" is a fundamental dynamic.

Then the combination of the "4" and the "3" (mathematically their multiplication) would result in the "12".

IV 4. a) The Zodiac

The "4·3=12" structure of the zodiac can be clearly seen:

The structure of the zodiac					
		Element			
		Fire	*Water*	*Air*	*Earth*
dynamics	*cardinal*	Aries	Cancer	Libra	Capricorn
	fixed	Leo	Scorpio	Aquarius	Taurus
	mutable	Sagittarius	Pisces	Gemini	Virgo

However, this order does not tell too much about the origin and the inner structure of the nature of the four elements.

The character of the four elements in the human psyche can be simply stated:

- Fire   = action   → strength
- Water   = feelings   → love
- Air   = thoughts   → truth
- Earth   = body   → thriving

It can be said, after all, that fire and air are related – they form the fire/air hexagon in the zodiac, whose signs are connected by the conjunction, sextile, trine and opposition, that is, by the connecting aspects.

106

The water and earth signs are also connected by these aspects and form the second hexagon.

However, the zodiac signs of these two groups have to each other only the separating aspects quincunx, square and semisextile.

Thus, among the four elements, there is the fire/air group and the water/earth group, both of which are relatively independent.

=> Here the four elements fire, water, air and earth are the basis of the twelve parts of a circle.

Fire and air are related to each other; water and earth are related to each other.

IV 4. b) The Elementary Particles

The same form of grouping exists in the twelve elementary particles:

- There are the two heavy quarks (up-quark, down-quark) and the two light particles (electron, neutrino) thus two groups of two.

- Also these four particles appear in three states or sizes.

The assignment of the two quarks as well as the electron and the neutrino to the two element pairs fire/air and water/earth is still uncertain. Do the two quarks correspond to the two heavy elements water and earth, since they are the two heavy particles in this group?

The formation of two groups seems to be an essential element in the "4".

=> Here again four basic elements appear in three sizes and thus form twelve particles.

They also form two pairs: the two quarks, which are heavy; and the two electron and neutrino, which are very light compared to the quarks.

IV 4. c) The Cardinal Points

When mentioning the "4" one thinks of course immediately of the four cardinal points and the seasons connected with them. The four elements can be assigned to them quite easily:

East	- spring	- air	(new beginning)
South	- summer	- fire	(heat)
West	- autumn	- water	(rain, fruits)
North	- winter	- earth	(rest, cold)

This overview can be completed by the times of day and the phases of life of a person:

East	- spring	- air	- morning	- birth
South	- summer	- fire	- noon	- life
West	- autumn	- water	- evening	- death
north	- winter	- earth	- night	- afterlife

This is a nice mandala, which can be completed by many other analogies like "blossom – fruit – ripeness – baldness" etc. This mandala probably plays a big role in rituals since the early Neolithic Age at the latest, but this mandala does not help much in understanding the four elements.

One can arrange the four elements in a four-divided circle – but this arrangement of the elements in it actually does not say much about the inner structure of the four elements. One can only say that air and fire are light and increase heat and that water and earth are heavy and decrease heat.

=> Here the four elements appear as a circle, as an endless sequence of four different states.

Again, fire/air and water/earth form two groups.

IV 4. d)   The States of Aggregation

There are four states of aggregation, which designate four clearly distinguishable physical states. These states correspond quite closely to the four elements.

    1. solid:
- The individual atoms are firmly and immovably bonded together.
- The energy level in this atomic bond is quite low.
- The solid state corresponds to the element earth.

2. liquid:

- The individual atoms are bonded together, but they are constantly changing the atoms to which they are bonded. Thus, the bond keeps the atoms together in a community, but this community is mobile.
- The energy level in this atomic bond is slightly higher than in the solid state.
- The liquid state of matter corresponds to the element water.

3. gaseous:

- The individual atoms are independent of each other and have no bonds to each other.
- The energy level in this atomic bond is high.
- The gaseous state of aggregation corresponds to the element air.

4. plasma:

- The electrons of the individual atoms have separated and now form a freely moving electron cloud within which the atomic nuclei move.
- The energy level in this atomic compound is very high.
- The plasma-like state of aggregation corresponds to the element fire.

=> Here the two states of aggregation solid (earth) and liquid (water) appear related (low energy level).

Likewise the two aggregate states gaseous (air) and plasma (fire) appear as related (high energy level).

This corresponds to the classical description of the four elements: Fire and Air are the two hot elements(high energy); Water and Earth are the two cold elements (low energy).

IV 4. e) The Square

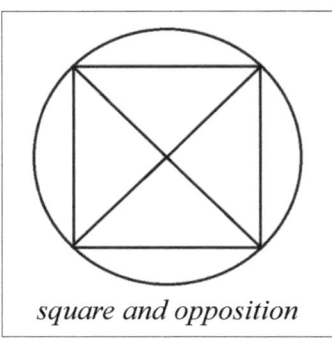

square and opposition

The "4" is, of course, closely related to the astrological square. If you draw four continuous squares (angles of 90°) in the zodiac, you get a geometrical square in a circle. The two pairs of opposite corners of the square can be connected by two diagonals, which are astrologically seen two oppositions.

So the four squares result from the combination of two oppositions. Interestingly, one of these two oppositions always connects a fire and an air sign, while the other opposition always connects a water and an earth sign. These two opposition cross at an angle of 90°.

Since the bipolar opposition corresponds to the likewise bipolar electromagnetic force, it looks as if the character of the "4" would result from the combination of a pair of "2". Does this mean that the character of the "4" is an offshoot of the "2", a derivation from it, a secondary formation?

=> Again, the two pairs of fire/air and water/earth appear, which seem to be a basic division of the four elements.

The square results from the combination of two oppositions.

IV 4. f) The Photon

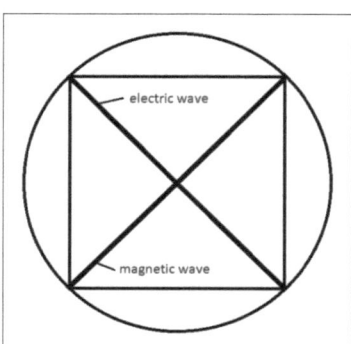

electric wave and magnetic wave (view from the front)

If you look for two intersecting oppositions in nature, you will find the photon. The photon, i.e. a light particle, can be represented as two waves: an electric wave and, at right angles to it, a magnetic wave.

If the electric wave has a wave crest, i.e. high energy, the magnetic wave has a wave trough, i.e. low energy – and if the magnetic wave has a wave crest, i.e. a high energy, the electric wave has a wave trough, i.e. low energy. The energy alternates back and forth between these two waves.

In the diagram on the left, the electric wave is one diagonal and the magnetic wave is the other diagonal. The diagram shows the two waves from the front, that is, from the point of view of an observer toward whom the light is traveling.

If you look at the light beam from the side, it looks like in the following diagram:

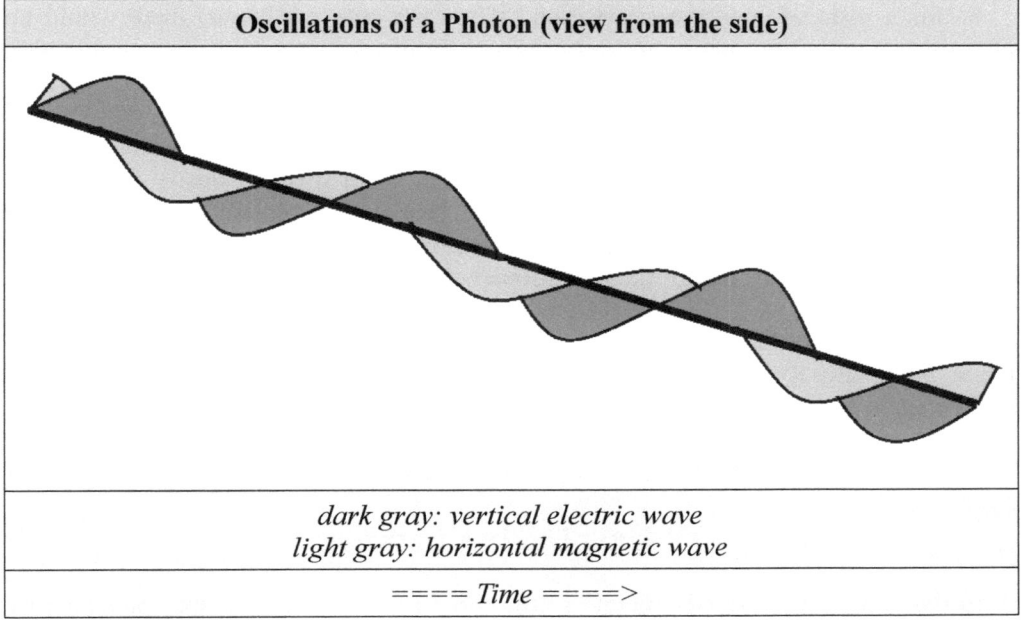

Oscillations of a Photon (view from the side)

dark gray: vertical electric wave
light gray: horizontal magnetic wave

==== *Time* ====>

So the energy in the electromagnetic wave changes constantly from the electric wave to the magnetic wave and back again – they have alternately their maximum (peak of the arc) and their minimum ("0", the axis).

In the following graph, the diagonal from top left to bottom right is the electric wave and the diagonal from top right to bottom left is the magnetic wave. The thick bar indicates where just the energy is to be found.

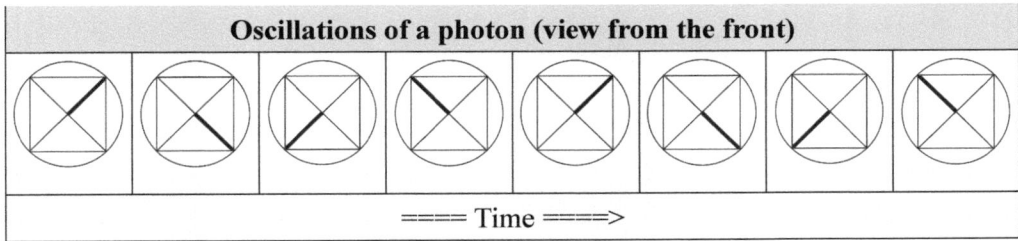

Oscillations of a photon (view from the front)

==== Time ====>

111

Why is that? Why is there not only one single wave? Why are there two coupled waves? And why do they also have two different effects, i.e. the electric and the magnetic field?

Is this a form of energy conservation? If it were only one wave, there would be alternately maximum energy and zero energy in this wave – with the combination between two waves, the fluctuation in the total energy of both waves is only about half as large.

The electric charge is bipolar. When an electric charge moves, the magnetic force, also bipolar, is created. The right angle between them then creates a quadrupolar force. Thus the "multiplication of polarities", which has already been mentioned several times, results in "$1 \cdot 3 \cdot 4 = 12$". The weak interaction with its (bipolar) electric charge would thus be a part of the electromagnetic force.

=> The light consists of two crossed "oppositions": the electric wave and in a right angle (90° angle) to it the magnetic wave.

Here again four poles are found in two groups (two waves).

IV 4. g) The Two Hexagons

In the zodiac there is the triangle of the three fire signs, which are connected by trines. The triangle of the three air signs is connected to the fire triangle by sextiles and oppositions. The hexagon of the fire and air signs is thus joined by sextiles, trines and oppositions to form an organic structure. It is a group with several characteristics: it pulsates (oppositions), it has a dynamic of development (trines) and its members stimulate each other (sextiles).

The same is true for the second group of zodiac signs, which consists of the three water signs and the three earth signs. They also form an organic group (a hexagon in the zodiac) with a solid inner cohesion.

The conjunction represents the identity of each astrological sign.

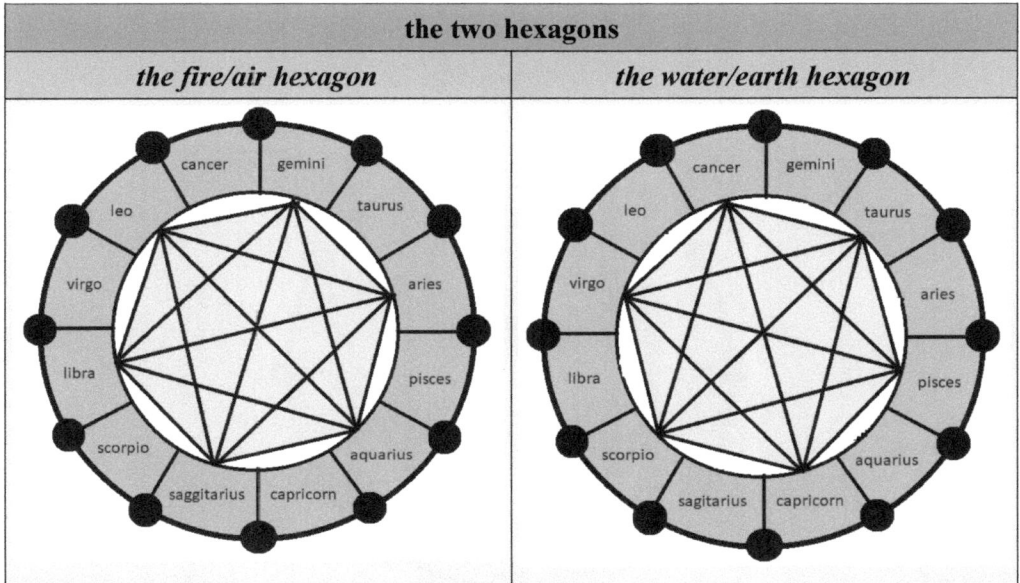

the two hexagons	
the fire/air hexagon	*the water/earth hexagon*

However, the two groups have among themselves only the aspects semisextile (advancement), square (separation) and quincunx (transformation). Consequently, these two groups do not form a superior organic unity, but two groups which separate themselves from the other group (square), transform themselves through the influence of the other group (quincunx) and develop further under its influence (semisextile).

By the "1" of gravitation (conjunction), the "2" of electromagnetic force (opposition) and the "3" of color force (trine) the two groups of six can be produced: "$1 \cdot 2 \cdot 3 = 6$".

To get from the group of six to the group of twelve of the zodiac, however, the separating, transforming and evolving qualities of square, quincunx and semisextile are obviously necessary.

One should therefore be able to assume that these qualities are connected with the four elements – as a relation between fire/air and water/earth.

the two hexagons
the connection *between the fire/air hexagon and the water/earth hexagon*

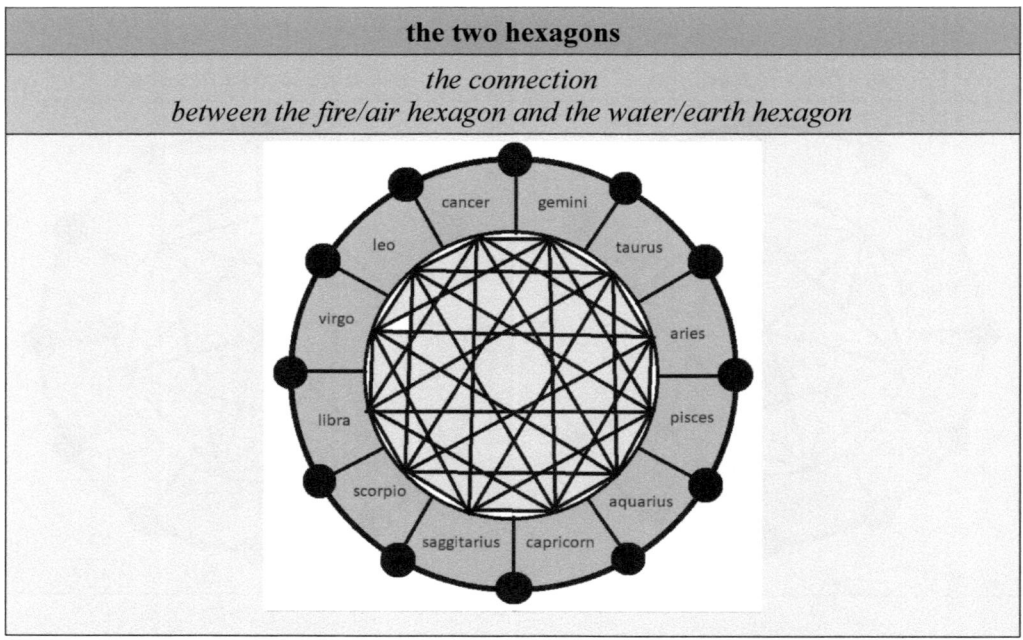

=> Fire/air and water/earth are separated from each other, transform each other and develop each other.

IV 4. h)   The Weak Interaction

The weak interaction occurs only in the atomic nucleus, because like the color force it has only a very small range.

In contrast to the other three forces, the weak interaction cannot produce a bond, but can (apart from an exchange of energy and momentum) only cause the decay and thus the transformation of atomic nuclei.

The weak interaction corresponds from its effect consequently to the three aspects square, quincunx and semisextile:

114

1. square:
    - The weak interaction makes a neutron decay into a proton and an electron.

    But it can also decay a proton into a neutron and a positron.

    Here two particles are separated, which corresponds to the quality of the square.

    The separating character of the square ("tent pole") also prevents the weak interaction like the three basic forces (gravitation, electromagnetic force, color force) from creating a bond between two particles.

2. semisextile:
    - The atom, in whose nucleus a neutron has changed into a proton, has now one proton more in the nucleus than before and has thus become another chemical element.

    Here one atom is transformed into another atom, which corresponds to the development quality of the semisextile.

3. quincunx:
    - The weak interaction does not adhere to the parity (symmetries) in physics, which is never violated by the three fundamental forces. (The parity will be explained in more detail below.)

    Here the quincunx becomes effective, which dissolves and restores order and which dissolves and restores tension. The quincunx disturbs the general order.

The action of a force can be described by the exchange of a particle. This is also true for the weak interaction:

- gravitation:	graviton
- electromagnetic force:	photon (light)
- color force:	gluon
- weak interaction:	Z^0 boson, W^+ boson, W^- boson

The peculiarity of the bosons of the weak interaction is that, unlike the other exchange particles, they can have an electric charge (W^+ boson, W^- boson). These bosons are obviously related to the electromagnetic force. This assumption had already resulted from the previous considerations: The square contains two oppositions (electromagnetic force).

The range of the weak interaction is limited to the atomic nucleus, because its exchange particles have a large mass in contrast to the exchange particles of the other three basic forces.

The strength of the weak interaction lies between the strength of gravitation and the strength of the electromagnetic force – its strength is closest to the strength of the electromagnetic force, to which it is related:

The relative Strength of the Basic Forces	
Force	*Relative Strength*
gravity	1
weak interaction	10^{26}
electromagnetic force	10^{37}
color force	10^{39}

A special feature of the weak interaction is that it is the only force that can violate the so-called "parity", i.e. (to put it very simply) that it can disturb symmetries.[9]
The parity says,

1. that a physical process can also run mirror-inverted (an experimental setup with a left-turning process should be mirror-inverted to the same experimental setup with a right-turning process, but otherwise identical to it);

2. that the particles involved in a process can also be replaced by their antiparticles or that all charges can be converted into their opposite; and

3. that a process can also be run backwards in time.

If the parity is preserved, the new experimental setup continues to behave completely normally: All particles adhere to the usual laws of nature and everything proceeds as it did before the transformation of one aspect of the experimental setup into its reflection, i.e. into its opposite.

However, the weak interaction, unlike all other forces, does not adhere to these three parities.

The three parities ("symmetries") are the intrinsic rotation of the particles, the charge of the particles (electromagnetic force, color force) and the direction of time.

9 An easily interpretable description of parity and its violation by the weak interaction may be found on youtube: "Veritasium: This Particle breaks Time-Symmetrie".

"Normally" the reflection of one of these three quantities has no influence on the physical process. The mirroring of these three quantities remains without any consequences in processes, which are determined only by the gravitation, the electromagnetic force and the color force – the symmetry remains.

The processes, which are shaped only by these three forces, obviously correspond to one of the hexagons in the zodiac, in which all signs of the zodiac work together harmonically. Astrologically, in such a hexagon, only conjunctions, oppositions, trines and sextiles act.

The weak interaction, which can violate the parity, i.e. the three symmetries "rotation, charge, time", is obviously the connecting link between the two hexagons in the zodiac – especially since the weak interaction by its nature also corresponds exactly to the semisextile, the square and the quincunx.

=> The weak interaction is the force which connects the two groups of two of the four elements (fire/air and water/earth).

IV 4. i) The d-Orbital

In electrons, there is a form of orbital in which the four electrons form the corners of a square. It is called the "d-orbital".

IV 4. j) Summary

The "4" of the four elements is a quality not immediately obvious. It has several facets:

- The "4" is the astrological square, that is, the separation.

- The "4" is the combination (intersection at a 90° angle) of two oppositions.

- The "4" is not only the 90° angle of the square (separation), but also the 150° angle of transformation and the 30° angle of further development.

- The "4" is the dynamic between the two hexagons on the zodiac, which is described by the three aspects square, quincunx and semisextile.

IV 5. Dynamics: Origin and Evolution

The basic statement of natural science is _"Every encounter between two things changes those two things in a predictable way."_

The basic statement of magic is "Like acts on like." or somewhat more precisely, _"Analogous things develop analogously to each other."_

A unified model of the world would have to combine these two basic principles into a single picture.

The difference between the two worldviews can be illustrated by a simple model. Both worldviews assume a primordial beginning: natural sciences assume a big bang and most magical-mythological worldviews assume a creation (often by a primordial god).

In both cases the world is homogeneous and undifferentiated before the creation, thus a unity.

The first step of the creation is the differentiation into two opposites.

> - At the big bang this primordial antithesis is the kinetic energy of the big bang (somewhat imprecisely the "big bang impulse") and the gravitational energy – thus the expanding motion and the contracting motion. One can also consider the emergence of the first particle together with its antiparticle as this primordial opposition pair.
>
> The sum of the primordial antithesis (e.g. "+1" and "−1") is always "0", otherwise something would have been created from nothing, which should be impossible because of the conservation laws. The mathematical-physical "formula" for the creation is therefore _"0 = (+1) + (−1)"_.

> - In the creation stories this primordial antagonism is e.g. with the Chineses Yin and Yang, with the Teutons fire and ice or in Mesopotamia and Egypt earth and water or earth god and sky goddess.
>
> The magic-mythological "formula" for the creation is therefore _"Tao = Yin + Yang"_. Here Yin and Yang are also exactly equal and therefore as sum again neutral ("0").

The first step in the origin of the world looks therefore the same in the physical and in the magic-religious world view. One can represent it as follows simplified graphically:

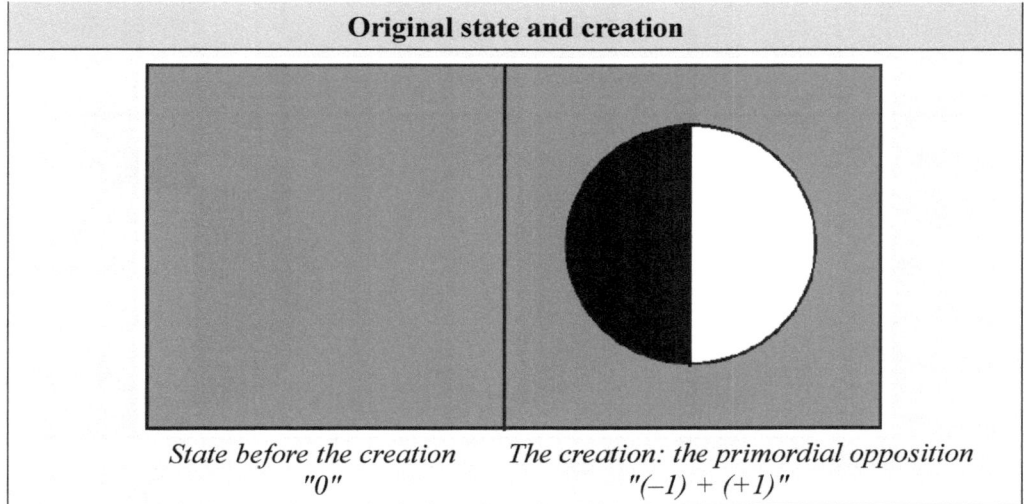

Original state and creation

State before the creation
"0"

The creation: the primordial opposition
"(–1) + (+1)"

While the original state and the first step are still the same in both world views, a clear difference appears in the second step.

In the natural-scientific world views the primordial antagonism differentiates itself further in a "diffuse" way, while the differentiation in the magic-mythological world views follows an overall pattern, by which a mandala develops, in which each part has a meaningful relation to all other parts.

In the physical world view the conservation laws are valid, which say that there is to every event a balancing event, i.e. that e.g. no matter can originate without antimatter or that not only the earth influences the course of the moon, but also the moon influences the course of the earth. The oldest formulation of this principle is "actio = reactio".

This principle is hardly considered in magic. But in magic the "conservation law of analogies", e.g. the conservation of the analogous order of the universe is always maintained.

This difference between the physical and the magic world views can be represented again in a simple way graphically:

119

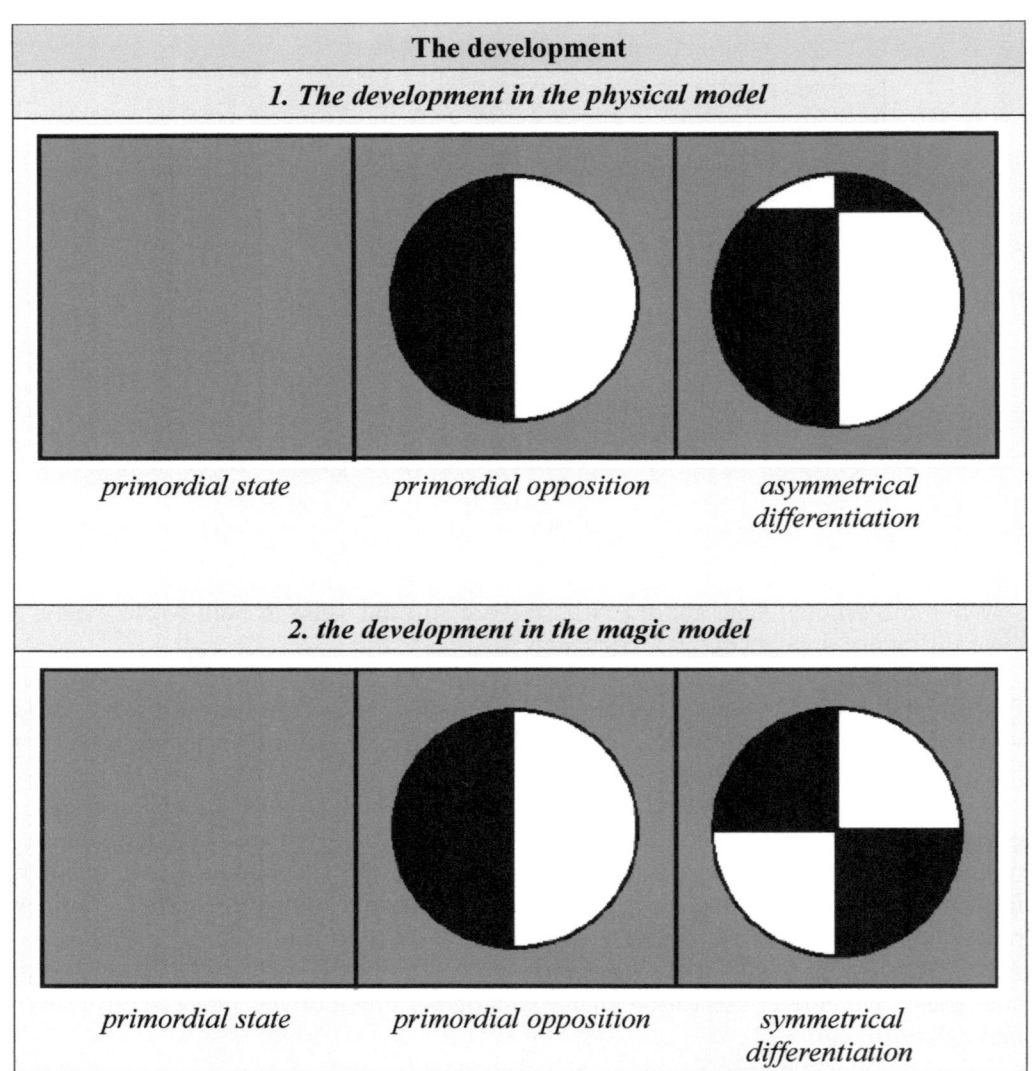

The interesting point of this difference is, that the magic-mythological model does not contradict the physical model, but only introduces another element into the description: The differentiation does not proceed randomly, but symmetrically.

In the magic-mythological model this symmetrical differentiation is not only an "aesthetic aspect", but it is also a possibility of effect, because the symmetry in this model is, so to speak, compellingly present – these are the "analogies", "equivalences" and "correspondences", which play such a big role in magic.

This symmetry can be preserved only if every time something changes in one place in the symmetrical structure of the world, things also change in a corresponding way in all other places of the world which correspond to this place.

Since one must assume a multi-layered superposition of all these analogous changes in the extremely complex world, it is not possible at first to recognice these analogous developments in a direct way in their whole complexity.

Only if one has a defined frame by a magical action like e.g. the drawing of a tarot card, within which one can observe the analogies, these correspondences e.g. between the tarot card and the events, to which the question to the tarot oracle refers, become obvious.

One can also describe these analogies in their temporal aspect: *"Each part is in a developmental coupling with all other parts with the same quality."*

The meaning of this phrase can best be seen in astrology: The planets move in fixed orbits around the Sun at fixed speeds. When one has found out the qualities of the planets, the angles between them, as well as the signs of the zodiac and the astrological houses, one has a reference system that develops in a predictable way and from which one can therefore read future developments.

These considerations show that, first of all, the only additional assumption necessary to describe magic together with natural sciences in a common world view is the assumption of a symmetrical differentiation and development of the world. This form of the development is not immediately noticeable only because the world is so large and complex.

If one assumes that the "symmetrical development" of the world exists, this would describe in a simple way such things as the functioning of oracles or the effect of wishes.

Also the "override" of natural laws e.g. with firewalking would mean only that the magic analogy effect is stronger in this case than the physical causal effect.

The trigger of the analogy effect at a firewalk is the confidence in the possibility to walk over the embers with healed feet. An essential function in firewalking is the role model, i.e. a person who demonstrates that it is possible. This person can then be referred to afterwards.

One can trace back this tradition over the medieval fire tests and the firewalks of the Druids and ever further – but who discovered this possibility first and by what means, is of course unknown. One can extend the traditionally handed down possibility of walking over the embers of course also independently e.g. to a naked lying in the embers or to a "cherry pit spitting" with pieces of embers. (Both are no mere theory, but my own experience.)

This possibility to create an analogy to someone or something is the reason why in almost all magical-mytholgical traditions there is learning of meditation and magic through a teacher – learning from a role model is the easiest, because in doing so one can step into analogy with the teacher.

The difference between the further development of the world in the two world views of physics and magic can be illustrated by the following graphic:

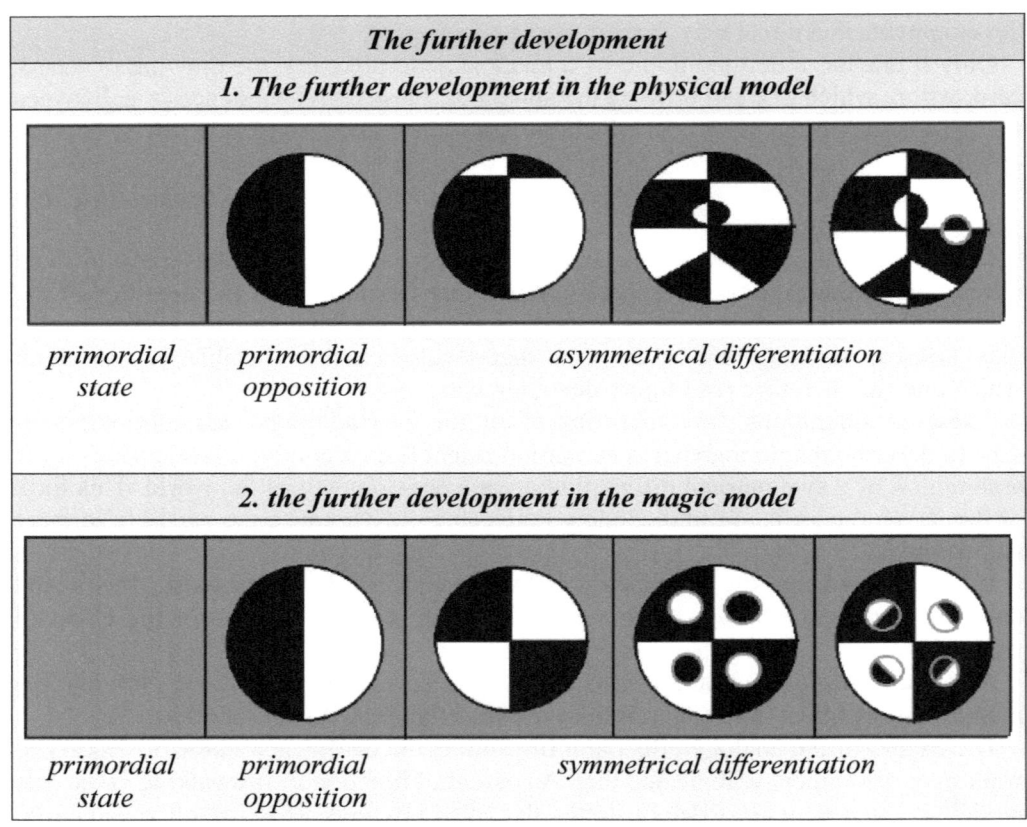

The considerations of the angles, the structure and the dynamics of the "12", the "three-step" etc. in earlier chapters show that the world can at least not have unfolded completely asymmetrically.

Moreover, if one considers that astrology describes the entire, complex processes on earth, it seems almost inevitable that one assumes a symmetrical unfolding of the world, for how else could the complex order of astrology be present in the world?

- - -

The cosmology, that is the combination of nuclear physics and astronomy, could prove that the universe has expanded within the first 10^{-32} seconds with a multiple of the speed of light. Here it is not matter which moves in the space-time, but it is the space-time itself which expands here – therefore a speed of far more than the speed of light is possible.

This process is called "inflationary universe", thus "fast expanding universe".

Also in many creation stories the creation goes on very fast in comparison with the duration of the subsequently existing world – God needed only seven days for it.

When one undertakes dream journeys to the area on the Kabbalistic Tree of Life that represents Creation (Chokmah), one experiences a storm of light that is a representation of Creation as a vision.

This correspondence of the "explosive creation" in both world views is, of course, no real proof of the correctness of the considerations in this book, since it is here only about the comparison of the physical cosmology with the creation myths, but not about a prescient analogy.

But as an addition to the points already considered, this correspondence is nevertheless quite pleasing.

IV 6.   Dynamics: Space and Time

Space and time are the basis of all physics and they are also an important element in magic-religious worldviews.

In particular, the question of the nature of time is of great importance in both world views. It appears in physics as space-time and in magic and mythology, among other things, as dream-time.

"Dreamtime" is a term that describes direct inner perception, i.e. dream travel, telepathy, foreseeing the future, and the like.

IV 6. a)   Physics: The Foundation

Spacetime is the foundation of physics:

- Humans are made of organs.
- Organs consist of cells.
- Cells (i.e. all living beings) consist of molecules.
- Molecules (i.e. all things) consist of atoms.
- Atoms consist of the nucleus and the electron shell.
- Atomic nuclei consist of protons and neutrons.
- Protons and neutrons consist of three quarks each.
- Quarks and electrons (and neutrinos) are "condensed energy".
- "Condensed energy" are energy quanta.
- Energy quanta are curvatures ("mountains" and "valleys") of space-time.
- Everything is space-time and its curvatures.

Space-time is the actual real thing – it is all that really exists. All large forms from the atom up to a human being or a sun are built up from the curvatures of space-time.

IV 6. b)   Physics: Time

What is time? First of all, it is a physical quantity that can be measured. It describes the sequence of events, i.e. the speed of the event or the change of this speed (acceleration). It is difficult to describe time without concepts of time like "velocity" and "acceleration" …

What is the relationship of time to space? Space exists and is everywhere, but it changes, because something happens in it constantly. It is possible to conceive of space as a void in which something happens, but since all things are ultimately curvatures of space-time, it is not actually reasonable to separate space from what happens in it. Space, then, is that which is constantly changing.

Through these changes, time becomes visible: a moment is identical with itself, unchanged, always the same. The succession of moments in which the world is in constantly new states shows that time exists.

One can be always only in one place of the time: Does this mean that one always sees only the momentary point of time, while time exists as a whole (past, present, future)? Or does it mean that only the moment is real?

If only the moment is real and exists, then space is the real thing and time is only a description of its changes. If time as a whole is real, then space is an record of time that is divided into moments.

The fact that space and time are inseparable and form the four dimensions of our world suggests that the extension of time into the past and into the future are as real as the extension of space.

However, this is an area of physics that is still largely unexplored.

If the assumption should be true that time is, so to speak, eternal and real as a whole, this would still mean that the normal waking consciousness is restricted to the present and perceives only the present – but this would not automatically be true for the other states of consciousness than the waking concsiousness.

Since ecstasy is one-pointed, it will presumably also perceive only the present moment. Deep sleep is silent and empty and therefore does not come into question for an expansion of consciousness into past and future. So only the subconscious remains, which is a promising candidate for "consciousness time travel" because 1st of the possibility of dream travel, 2nd the coupling to the collective subconscious and 3rd the ability to remember.

IV 6. c) Physics: The Speed of Light

Since space-time is the foundation of all physical phenomena, it is not surprising that the combination of space and time, i.e. speed, is a central element of physics. The velocity is the distance a mass moves uniformly in a given time – this is then expressed, for example, in "meters per second", in "kilometers per hour" or in "miles per day".

Since Einstein it is known that the speed of light is the limit for the speed of masses and energies in our world.

But the speed of light is also the central transformation quantity:

- Energy can "condense" to mass, whereby the energy shrinks by "c^2". This is described by the famous formula "$E = m \cdot c^2$". The "condensing" of energy to mass would then look as follows: "$E:c^2=m$". The transformation of mass into energy (as e.g. in an atomic bomb explosion) looks like this: "$m \cdot c^2 = E$".

Pure energy like light has no fixed form: Two light beams can cross without affecting each other — light does not collide with light. Light can therefore move completely freely as long as it only encounters other light (which can happen to a light ray in space for many millions of years).

A light quantum (photon) has no solid shell. However, from sufficiently many photons, by the "condensation" of energy to mass, e.g. an electron can be created, which has a solid shell. The "c^2" obviously changes into the solid shell of the electron (or another particle with mass).

- The same process exists another time: If mass turns into the substance of a black hole, the mass "condenses" again with the help of the factor "c^2". If energy turns into the substance of a black hole, this would happen with the factor "$c^2 \cdot c^2 = c^4$". This "c^4" is therefore also the central factor with the mathematical-physical description of a black hole.

The "c^2" is the conversion factor of energy into mass and of mass into the substance of a black hole. In both cases, a part of the mobility of the initial substance is lost and a shell is created around the new substance. (The black hole is "black" because not even light can get through its "shell" to the outside.)

Why is this transformation factor a velocity? This can only mean that the space-time is that in which something "condenses" during this transformation. What happens during these transformations must be something that gives a new quality to the curvatures of space-time.

IV 6. d) Magic: Astrology

Like in physics, time itself has already been explored very thoroughly in magic — of course in a completely different way.

Like all magical phenomena, the "magical time phenomena" described here are only a relevant part of one's world view if one has already experienced them oneself.

Something you don't know yourself, you can't use as part of the foundation of your own world view.

With the help of astrology it is possible not only to describe the character of a person, but also to predict the course of a person's life and also the future events that will affect the whole community. So, from the point of view of astrology, the quality of the future is already determined in the present.

Also the fact that one can describe already today the horoscope of a person precisely, who will be born only in the future e.g. on 20. 8. 2037 at 17.14 o'clock in Berlin, shows that the future time qualities are already fixed.

A newborn also does not receive its "astrological character" only in the moment of its birth – it develops during the nine months of the pregnancy towards that, what it is at the moment of its birth. The time of birth does not shape the human being – the horoscope at the time of birth merely makes it possible to calculate astrologically the quality of the human being in question.

One cannot conclude from these three observations that every future concrete event is already fixed today, but one can conclude that the future time qualities, which can be recognized and described astrologically, are already fixed today.

These qualities are located on the transition between consciousness and matter, which is often circumscribed as the "life force realm" and the "magic realm".

IV 6. e)   Magic: Foreseeing the Future

If you ask people about divination dreams, you will find that an astonishing number of people have dreamed something that happened the next day.

Using the Tarot or the I Ching to predict the future is quite popular. Also in this case, as in astrology, one first receives qualities as an answer.

However, one can use any oracle, including astrology, to go on from the quality one finds in it, through "inner listening", through a dream journey or the like, to predictions that are just as concrete as the divination dreams mentioned at the beginning.

With a little practice it is possible to perceive the future without any aid. This feels like remembering – one is looking only in the "other direction".

From this it can be concluded that also very concrete future events are already fixed today – which of course immediately leads to the question of personal freedom …

Its a difficult question: Has one foreseen the future by the inner picture or has one shaped and caused the future by the inner picture?

Basically, one can only say that the image one sees inwardly in the present has a connection with the future event. However, if one cannot distinguish the foreseeing from the magical causing, both should be the same. This means that one can only say that one's consciousness has a connection with the future events – whether causing or perceiving cannot be distinguished.

This distinction is again something that makes sense in the forst place from the physical point of view, because physics looks at developments along the time ray – there it makes a difference if one foresees something or if one causes something.

In magic, however, the connection between qualities is considered – and the inner picture in the present has a qualitative connection with the event in the future, because both are in analogy to each other. Here only the analogy is important and not the question "perception or causation?".

Thus, even when considering time, it is evident that physics considers quantities and that magic considers qualities.

IV 6. f) Magic: The Conversation with one's own Soul

There is a possibility to travel to one's own soul with the help of a dream journey and see one's entire future life. Of course, this is information that should not be taken lightly, because this knowledge changes your entire life: After that, one no longer has the freedom to choose what to do (the psyche's point of view), but only the freedom to choose how to experience it (the soul's point of view). The psyche is looking for happiness, the soul is looking for intensity …

This knowledge of the events in the rest of one's life that one can receive from one's own soul is a very convincing experience with regard to the determinacy of the future.

IV 6. g) Magic: Homeopathy

Homeopathic remedies do not act according to the chemical constituents of the substance from which they are made, but according to the history of that substance.

For example, Lycopodium helps with a certain type of "quiet depression." A typical Lycopodium patient is the lonely, aging notary who maintains himself and the law, but who feels that he is already in the movie credits of his life …

This is because during the Carbon Age, most of the plants on Earth have been lycopods – back then, the lycopod was the "king of the forests". From the tree trunks of these forests the hard coal, the brown coal, the oil and the natural gas developed. Today, however, the Lycopodium lives only as a small herb at the edge of the forest on the "mass graves" of its ancestors – its great time is over …

There are many examples for this connection between the history of a remedy and the homeopathic effect of this remedy.

Among other things, this example shows that Lycopodium has a memory – otherwise its effect could not correspond to its history.

The "green thumb" and many plant experiments show that plants also react to thoughts. Therefore, plants must also have a consciousness – since a consciousness is inevitably formed from the combination of perception (sensing thoughts) and memory.

Homeopathy shows that there is a "non-material memory" in animals, plants and minerals (from which the homeopathic remedies are made) that goes back millions of years. From this, one can conclude with great probability two things:

> 1. The human beings as a collective have also such a non-material memory: the collective subconsciousness.

> 2. It is quite probable that this "non-material bridging from the present to the past" can also function as "bridging from the present to the future".

This would show once again that time from the magical point of view consists of past, present and future at the same time, and that the waking consciousness, which is anchored in the present, can extend with the help of the unconsciousness (dream journeys and the like) to the past and presumably also to the future.

From a magical point of view, time appears as a continuum in which all moments exist simultaneously and in which (sub-)consciousness can travel to all moments in time.

IV 6. h) Magic: Reincarnation

The memories of past lives, which, if they are detailed enough, can be subsequently checked for their correctness, is ultimately nothing other than the "non-material memory" that becomes apparent through the action of some homeopathic remedies.

It is true that one cannot say with certainty whether one has reincarnated, that is, whether one's own soul has "been on earth" in this life and in a previous life. But one can at least say that it is possible to grasp the life of a former person from today – there are plenty of examples of this.

The possibility to learn from one's own soul how the rest of one's life will be is very similar to this memory.

From the usual physical point of view one asks the obvious question whether one has really been this "person 200 years ago" or whether one can get only telepathically the information about this person's life. However, this distinction is interesting only if one considers the world as a course of events along the time ray.

From the magical point of view, one would only ask if there is an analogy between the consciousness today and the consciousness of the "man 200 years ago". If one can remember the life of the man of that time, there is obviously a connection.

If one can also see that one's own life today and the life of the person back then have a qualitative correspondence, one has gone one step further: One's own life today and the life of the person back then are analogies to each other.

In what does one see one's own identity in one's present life? That decides about the interpretation of reincarnation:

> - If one sees one's own identity in one's own psyche, the identity is limited to the present life, because one cannot have led a corresponding life before – the horoscopes and the historical circumstances are too different for that.

> - If one sees one's identity in one's own soul, one can look at what soul the person of that former time had – is it the same soul as the one one has today? If that is true, then it makes sense to speak of the person of that time as one's own previous incarnation. If this is not true, then one should speak of a telepathic memory of the life of another person – in which case it would be interesting to ask why one can remember the life of just this person …

IV 6. i) Magic: God and Gods

In almost all myths the gods and goddesses live eternally – and the one God is virtually timeless.

On the Tree of Life, the one God corresponds to Kether, the initial unity – in terms of superstring theory, Kether is time itself. God in the sense of the primordial unity of the world, that is, the Only-All-One, is eternal and unchanging.

The Gods and Goddesses, on the other hand, correspond to the first triangle below Kether on the Tree of Life. The three areas of this triangle are designated by the Hebrew names "Chokmah", "Binah" and "Da'ath". The deities correspond to the three spatial dimensions. They have a history, different characteristics, relationships among themselves, etc.

At least in this context, it is clear that time is the origin of creation and that space is a part of creation: The gods are aspects of God.

IV 6. j) Comparison

In physics, space-time appears as the foundation of the world. It is at least conceivable that time is eternal and that we always experience only a single point in time with our waking consciousness in the respective moment – but that it must not be impossible in principle to directly perceive other points in time than the present.

In magic such consciousness-time-travels are quite common, as prophetic dreams, oracles, time-dream-journeys, homeopathy, reincarnation-memories etc. make clear.
Astrology also shows very vividly that at least the qualities of time are qualitatively fixed in a very differentiated way long before their occurrence as a concrete event.
However, the possibility of foreseeing the future makes it clear that also the very concrete future events and not only the quality of these future events are already fixed now.

Also with the consideration of the time it shows up that physics always examines quantities and the magic always examines qualities:
Physical time phenomena are also best described with the help of quantities, such as the speed of light.
On the other hand, magical time-phenomena are best described with the help of qualities like the analogy between the waking consciousness of a present-day man and his memory of the life of a man who died a long time ago.

IV 7. Remarkable physical phenomena

There are still a number of physical phenomena, which have no direct magical correspondence or consciousness correspondence, but are nevertheless interesting for the topic of this book, since they let individual aspects of the connections between consciousness and matter and/or between physics and magic become clearer.

IV 7. a) Wave/Particle Duality

This principle states that all physical particles can behave both like a solid particle and like a wave. This shows vividly the correctness of the famous formula "$E = m \cdot c^2$", because "E" (energy) is a boundaryless wave and "m" (mass) is a solid particle.

The particles behave like a wave when they can move freely, but like a particle when they collide with other particles.

IV 7. b) Decay probabilities

The direct proof of acausal processes within physics is an important element for the formulation of a unified world view, since magic and mythology are based on just such acausal processes.

Historically, the first major discovery of an acausal physical process was the decay of elementary particles, which does not follow a fixed causal rule, but merely has a certain fixed random distribution.

Einstein has always doubted this purely statistical rule, by which it cannot be predicted for the individual case, how a particle will decay ("God does not throw dice."), because he considered it inconceivable that there are processes which are not causally determined.

In the decay of particles certain relations between the possible kinds of decay occur. Some particles always decay in the same way, others half one way and half another, for still others there are three possibilities, one of which occurs in half the cases and the other two in a quarter of the cases each, and so on.

If one looks at these decay probabilities, one finds that the proportions which the various decay types have are not completely arbitrary % figures such as 29%, 87% or 14%, but that they are proportions related to the "zodiacal angles":

Decay probabilities			
Share	*Fraction*	*angle*	*astrological aspect*
$\approx 100\%$	1	$360° = 0°$	Conjunction
$\approx 50\%$	1/2	180°	Opposition
$\approx 33\%$	1/3	120°	Trine
$\approx 67\%$	2/3	$240° = 2 \cdot 120°$	
$\approx 25\%$	1/4	90°	Square
$\approx 75\%$	3/4	$270° = 3 \cdot 90°$	
$\approx 17\%$	1/6	60°	Sextile
$\approx 8\%$	1/12	30°	Semisextile

Only the fraction of 42%, which corresponds to the fraction 5/12 and the angle of 150° and thus to the quincunx, seems to occur rather rarely.

One can of course say that it is just the simple fractions that are found in the decay proportions, but the correspondence with the astrological aspects is nevertheless there – and the simple fractions "1/5", "2/5", "3/5", "4/5", "1/7", "2/7", 3/7" etc. are also missing, which one should then expect.

This correspondence can probably best be regarded as a "supporting finding" for the world view sketched in this book, in which the angles corresponding to the astrological aspects play a major role.

IV 7. c)   Heisenberg's uncertainty relation

The Heisenberg uncertainty relation shows that the things of this world are no longer exactly defined at magnitudes far below the size of electrons. One cannot measure certain sizes at the same time. This is because the elementary particles are not solid spheres, but particles and waves at the same time.

The particles are finally "mountains" in the space-time … and from a mountain can be said exactly, where its summit is, but not, where it starts exactly below – the foot of the mountain goes gradually into the level, on which it stands.

The uncertainty relation has the same cause as the wave/particle dualism: The elementary particles have no sharp boundaries because they are "mountains" in space-time.

IV 7. d)   Virtual Particles

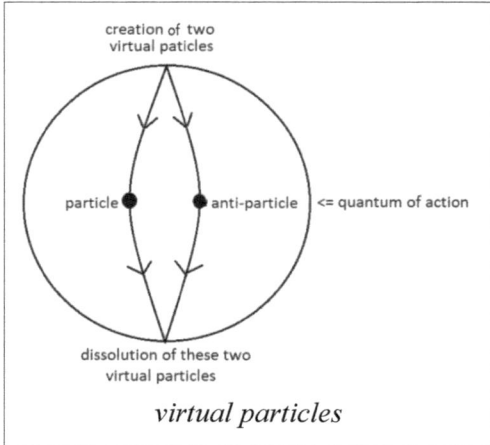

creation of two
virtual paticles

particle   anti-particle   <= quantum of action

dissolution of these two
virtual particles

virtual particles

In the range of the size of elementary particles and in even smaller size ranges very many random processes occur ("virtual particles"), which only have to keep within a certain frame (mass, lifetime etc.), but otherwise can do what they want.

Within a certain frame it is possible that a particle and its antiparticle, e.g. an electron and a positron, are created, exist for a moment and then unite and dissolve again.

One can represent this process also mathematically: "$0 = [(+1) + (-1)] = 0$". If one represents this equation as a temporal development, this looks as follows: "$0 \rightarrow [(+1) + (-1)] \rightarrow 0$".

In the realm of large things, you see nothing of this possibility – but in the realm of very small things, these virtual particles can arise together with their counterpart (antiparticles) completely randomly and without cause. All they have to do is observe a finite lifetime, which is smaller the larger the two virtual particles are, and observe the conservation laws, i.e. the opposite charge "$[(+1) + (-1)]$".

The causality is so to speak "smooth" and unambiguous in the range of large things, but "rough" and completely arbitrary within a fixed limit in the range of very small things.

One can think of these virtual particles in a simple way: If you look at a "mountain" in spacetime (=particle) and move closer and closer to this "mountain", you will eventually see that what looked like the smooth surface of a mountain from a distance are in fact completely jagged slopes and peaks. This does not change the fact that the mountain as a whole is "smooth" – it is only when viewed from close up that the many rocks and crevices become visible, which correspond to the restlessness of the virtual particles.

Thus the virtual particles only confirm again that the space-time is the basis of our world. And this space-time looks "smooth" seen from the distance, but seen from the near it is quite uneven, what becomes visible as "virtual particles".

Below the Planck size finally any form dissolves and one reaches a structureless and completely free area of this world. There are so many virtual particles at this magnitude that one can hardly see the "real particles".

If one remains in the mountain picture, one has now reached the mountain and digs with his hands in the sand in a hollow of this mountain and does not see the mountain as a whole any more.

The sub-Planck area, which is also called quite figuratively "quantum foam" (quanta = particles), is no longer structured by causality, but certainly still by the conservation laws and possibly also by probabilities.

This "freedom" of the virtual particles is an essential element of most magic-mythological world views.

However, one cannot conclude from the freedom of these virtual particles that also the big things like e.g. a human being is free. This freedom exists first of all only in the realm of very small quantities.

IV 7. e) Quantum Entanglement

The quantum entanglement is not only a structure, which agrees with the magic-mythological world views, but a physical process, which corresponds also exactly to the procedure in magic: Two things are connected with each other (in physical terms thus "entangled", in magic terms however "enchanted") and behave then afterwards analogously to each other:

- In quantum entanglement, quantum A behaves exactly like quantum B, which has been coupled with quantum A (e.g. two parts of a laser beam).

- In the Woodoo-doll spell, a person suffers exactly what is inflicted on the doll that embodies him.

IV 7. f) Antiparticles

Antiparticles are particles that are like a "normal" particle but have opposite properties. For example, the positron resembles an electron, except that it has a positive and not a negative electric charge. With an antiparticle the mass, the life span and the spin (approximately the rotation) remain the same – only the charges of the electromagnetic force and the color force change.

There is to every particle also its antiparticle – in some cases, however, the antiparticle is identical with the particle itself, if the particle has no properties (charges) which can be turned into their opposite.

In physics the antiparticles are also understood as normal elementary particles which fly "abnormally" against the normal time direction. This gives rise to the assumption that also the foreseeing of the future, as it is known from magic, could be quite normal in the unified world view and could be connected with the antiparticles.

However, this interpretation of the antiparticles is still unexplored.

IV 7. g)   Acausal Connections

There are in some areas of physics events which happen exactly at the same time although they have no direct connection to each other. From the point of view of magic, one would naturally assume an analogy here, which leads to this simultaneity.

The most striking case is the simultaneous occurrence of the end of the thermal equilibrium and the emergence of the first electron shells 700 years after the big bang. The term "thermal equilibrium" means that during the first 700 years our universe was everywhere equally dense, equally hot and equally bright.

On the kabbalistic tree of life, however, these processes both belong to the transition called "trench" and are therefore analogous processes − which therefore occurred simultaneously.[10]

IV 7. h)   Elegance

The basic quality in the magical-mythological worldviews is rightness: all things are in their right place and behave there in the right way, resulting in simplicity, plainness, symmetry, rhythm, order, effectiveness and beauty.

This rightness is also the basic quality of every complex structure, because in it things are not arranged arbitrarily, but in a meaningful pattern.

In the last decades, this quality of "rightness" has also become familiar to mathematicians and physicists under the name "elegance". An old guideline among all researchers is, "The simplest possibility is also the most probable."

Through the physicist Brian Green, the term "elegance" has become popular for the observation that the mathematical model that is simplest and most symmetrical has the greatest chance of also being the most accurate model for describing a physical relationship.

---

10 A more detailed description may be found in my book „Blüten des Lebensbaumes I".

IV 7. i) Self-Similarity

A special aspect of elegance is self-similarity: In every system the same forms can be found as well in the details as in the overall appearance.

This self-similarity is naturally best known in man himself: Whether one "reads" his palm lines, uses the iris diagnosis, checks the foot reflex zones, uses the pulse diagnosis, or otherwise examines a part of the body more closely, one will always arrive at the same description of the human being – if one has studied the part of the body under consideration for a very long time and with many different people, and has therefore become competent.

The best known non-human self-similarity is probably a phenomenon that occurs in fractals. These are complex mathematical entities that can be represented graphically. If one magnifies a certain fractal form, such as the "heart shape" named after the mathematician Mandelbrot, more than a billion times, one eventually arrives at the "heart shape" again via very many other intermediate forms. The tiny Mandelbrot-form becomes visible as a detail through the magnification of the large Mandelbrot-form.

A simpler example is the observation that in many trees the shape of the whole plant coincides with the shape of a single leaf.

The most comprehensive example is the distribution of galaxies in space, which looks like foam: The water of the many bubbles of the foam corresponds to the galaxies; the air of the bubbles corresponds to the void between the galaxies. This foam-like distribution of galaxies in the universe corresponds again to the quantum foam structure at the Big Bang …

This self-similarity of systems is a clear indication that with the development of a system from its "egg cell" also structures co-determine the form, so that all parts of the whole have the same form and the same character at the end.

The same connection also results from astrology, since the birth horoscope of a person describes not only his lifestyle, but also his body and each individual body part. The horoscope is, so to speak, the individual plan for shaping the self-similarities of the person in question.

IV 8.   Remarkable Magic-Phenomena

In magic there are "normal" phenomena such as telepathy and telekinesis, which can be described with the help of analogies.

Phenomena like reincarnation memories and foreseeing the future require that analogies be understood not only spatially but also temporally: While telepathy sees something in the present and telekinesis moves something in the present, the connection of consciousness with something in the past or in the future is a temporal analogy that goes beyond the present.

There are two phenomena that at first sight seem to require a more complex explanation than merely „analogy": astral travel and violation of causality.

IV 8. a)   Astral Projection

In an astral journey, one leaves one's own physical body with one's consciousness and with one's perceptive faculty and returns to it after a while.

Here the consciousness as a whole connects with another place than the one where the physical body is at the moment.

IV 8. b)   "Violations of Causality"

In the case of materializations, firewalkings, levitations and transformations of things, as for example in the case of spiritual healings, it is shown that the consciousness can have so stong an influence on the course of events that physical rules are overruled.

Thus it becomes clear that the physical "laws" are in reality only a physical "inertia" of the events, which can be steered by a correspondingly high intensity of the consciousness to a completely differently effect than the physical laws let expect.

- - -

These considerations are of course rather abstract and only credible in a very limited way, if one has not experienced firewalks, spontaneous healings, materializations or similar.

But a book can't change that much – for that magic experiments ans experiences are necessary …

V The formulas of the unified world view

In the previous chapters the differences and the similarities of the physical world view and the magic world view have been considered. Three principles played the main role:

> 1. *"Consciousness is the inside of the world – matter is the outside of the world. Both are two sides of the same thing."*

> 2. *"The world is causally ordered – and the world is ordered by analogies. Both together create a kalaidoscopically unfolding symmetric order."*

> 3. *"The possibilities of magic and the imprints and cycles described by astrology on the one hand and the causality described by physics on the other hand can be traced back to the same basic principles."*

It would now be desirable to put the findings from the previous chapters into as simple, universally valid and easily understandable a form as possible.

V 1. "Inside = Outside"

The world can be experienced as consciousness – the world can be experienced as matter.

The experience of the world as consciousness is inside – the experience of the world as matter is outside.

Consciousness is described by magic, meditation, religion and psychology – matter is described by physics and the natural sciences based on it.

Inside and outside are different, but they are connected.

Both can act on each other – resulting in four types of effect:

> Matter → Matter: One stone bumps against another and makes it roll away.

> Matter → Consciousness: An event on the outside is perceived and becomes a memory.

> Consciousness → Matter: Someone feels hunger inside and therefore reaches for an apple outside.

> Consciousness → Consciousness: Someone retrieves a key lost by another by telepathy. Someone moves an object by telekinesis.

If one understands all elementary particles as a tube and also all interactions between all things as (smaller) tubes, the model of an all-encompassing tube system results.

The experience of the inside of these tubes is consciousness – this inside is open to every place in the tube system. One can go anywhere with one's consciousness through the inside of the tube, so to speak.

The experience of the outside of these tubes is matter – this outside is delimited to every other place of this tube system. One bumps, so to speak, everywhere against the outer surface of other places of this tube system.

V 2.   the angles

Each angle resulting from the division of the circle into units of 30° has a certain quality which is found in many places. This quality is the same wherever this angle occurs.

V 2. a)   The 0° Angle

The angle of 0° is the place where something is. This angle therefore embodies identity with itself – astrologically this is the conjunction that unites two things.

This angle must correspond to a force which is unipolar, thus pulling all things together – this is gravity.

This angle forms spherical shapes – everything is pulled together evenly. This is the round shape of suns, planets, moons, electron shells (s-orbital), atomic nuclei, etc.

V 2. b)   The 180° Angle

The angle of 180° is bipolar – it is like a swing, like an oscillation between two poles. Astrologically, this is the opposition that causes a swing between two poles.

As a force this is the electromagnetic force with its two electric poles "+" and "–" and its two magnetic poles "north" and "south".

One can also regard the big bang impulse and the gravitation as an opposite complementary pair. The p-orbitals of the electrons have the form of an opposition, i.e. approximately the form of a dumbbell.

This polarity is mainly known as "Yin and Yang". This opposition and the resulting dynamics are described in the I Ching, whose name means "Book of Changes". This primordial opposition also appears as a pair of primordial deities, as Earth God and Heaven Goddess, as Sulphur and Mercurius, as Fire and Ice, Water and Earth, etc.

V 2. c) The 120° Angle

The angle of 120° is tripolar – it is like a triangle. This is astrologically the trine that causes a strong bond between two things.

As a force, this is the color force that holds the three quarks together in a proton or in a neutron. It has three poles, called "red," "yellow," and "blue," which together make the neutral "white." The three sizes of the four elementary particles also belong to these groups of three.

In stone healing this angle is found in the trigonal crystals, whose effect is calming and integrating.

V 2. d) The 90° Angle

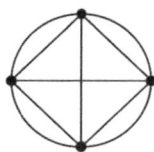

The angle of 90° is quadripolar – it is like a square. This is astrologically the square that holds two things apart like a tent pole, and by this "constructive separation" spans a space.

No physical force corresponds to this angle, but it is related to the weak interaction. But it is found e.g. as 90° angle between the electric wave and the magnetic wave in a photon. Also the Cartesian coordinate system, the four kinds of elementary particles and the d-orbitals of the electrons have a 90° angle, i.e. they form a cross.

In lithotherapy, the 90° angle is found in the cubic crystals, which have a bulky, forming, ordering and delimiting effect. This "right angle" also appears as the cardinal points and their symbolism.

V 2. e)   The 60° Angle

The angle of 60° is six-polar – it forms a honeycomb. Astrologically, this is the sextile that combines different but complementary elements into one group.

This angle does not correspond to any physical force. However, it is found, for example, as a 60° angle in honeycombs and snowflakes, in the angular spacing of two moons on the same orbit around a planet, in the most space-saving arrangement of identical elements, in the benzene ring, in quartzes, in the f-orbitals of electrons, and so on.

Crystals with a hexagonal crystal lattice have a calming, gregarious and group-forming effect in stone healing.

V 2. f)   The 30° Angle

The angle of 30° is twelve-polar – it forms the zodiac and the superstring. This is astrologically the semisextile, i.e. the progression towards the next state.

No physical force corresponds to this angle. It is not found, apart from the twelve division of the superstring and the zodiac, as an obvious 30° angle, but only as a "development-stimulating element" in the form of the igniting spark in physics, as a catalyst in chemistry and as an enzyme in biology.

This angle is also related to the weak interaction.

V 2. g)   The 150° Angle

Like the 30° angle, the 150° angle is twelve-polar – one returns to the starting point in the circle only after twelve steps of 150°. This is the astrological aspect of the quincunx, which causes constant change and requires constant rearrangement or retensioning.

This is the third angle, along with the square and the semisextile, that is related to the weak interaction. The weak interaction causes the decay of particles.

V 3. Some Connections and Distinctions

There are some connections between the structures and dynamics considered in the earlier chapters, whose closer examination will make clearer the total system of found qualities that appear both in physics and in magic/astrology.

V 3. a) 120° and 30°

Both the 120° angle and the 30° angle describe a further development. However, these two progressions are very different, so a more precise distinction is beneficial:

- The trine (120°) goes a big step further – the semisextile (30°) goes a small step further.

- The trine remains in its own element (e.g. fire: Aries – Leo – Sagittarius – Aries) – the semisextile always changes to an element foreign to it (e.g. from the fire of Aries to the earth of the Taurus following Aries).

- The 120° angle describes a close cohesion – the semisextile describes a transition to a completely different state.

The 120° angle is an organic change to a different alignment in the same system: the element (e.g. fire) remains the same, only the dynamic in which this element is located (cardinal, fixed or mutable) changes.

However, the 30° angle leads to a pause (from a fire/air sign to a water/earth sign) or to a departure (from a water/earth sign to a fire/air sign). There comes something completely new, a completely different mode, through which the previous step is developed further on.

V 3. b) 120° and Three-Step

The triangle and thus the astrological trine always consist of the three dynamics "cardinal, fixed and mutable". These three dynamics are identical with the three-step, on which, among other things, the chakra system and the Kabbalistic Tree of Life are based. These three dynamics show up in a simple form in all flow processes like in a fountain, in the convection current inside the sun, in the volcanoes and the continental drift on earth, in the Gulf Stream and the winds, in a bubbling soup pot, in the solar wind (solar wind, shock front, bow wave), in the three sizes of the elementary particles, in Kundalini Yoga (rising, unfolding and flowing down of the life force), in the three time deities etc.

This three-step dynamic characterizes all flow processes in organic systems. The three phases of this flow have the following character:

1st phase (cardinal): free, spontaneous, impetuous, self-determined, bundled, promoting, creating.

2nd phase (fixed): self-centered, outwardly delimiting, formative, contentious, rivaling, fleshing out, expanding, generalizing

3rd phase (mutable): perceiving, participating, caring, applying, cooperating, diverse

The three-step is identical with the three dynamics. The three dynamics are in turn the three corners of the triangle in the zodiac, which consists of three trines, that is, three 120° angles. A trine represents not only cohesion, but also the transition from one of the three dynamics to another.

Thus, the chakra system and the Kabbalistic Tree of Life are not two systems that stand independently next to the zodiac with the seven different angles in it, but they are both an application and differentiation of the 120° angle and its inner dynamics, that is, the organic unfolding.

V 3. c)   4 Elements and 90°

The three-step is identical with the three dynamics of one of the four elements – the 4 structures are the four elements in the same dynamic.

If you look at the three-step (three trines) in the zodiac, all three signs involved belong to the same element: either fire (Aries – Leo – Sagittarius), water (Cancer – Scorpio – Pisces), air (Libra – Aquarius – Gemini) or earth (Capricorn – Taurus – Virgo).

If you look at a square in the zodiac, all four signs have the same dynamic: either cardinal (Aries, Cancer, Libra, Capricorn) or fixed (Leo, Scorpio, Aquarius, Taurus) or mutable (Sagittarius, Pisces, Gemini, Virgo).

The four <u>cardinal signs</u> are like four people who want something different: to express themselves spontaneously (Aries), to feel spontaneously (Cancer), to think spontaneously (Libra) and to create something spontaneously (Capricorn).

The four <u>fixed signs</u> are like four people who have different points of view: expressing oneself unrestrictedly (Leo), feeling unrestrictedly (Scorpio), thinking unrestrictedly (Aquarius) and creating something unrestrictedly (Taurus).

The four <u>mutable signs</u> are like four people who want to take care of different things: expressing themselves in the whole world (Sagittarius), feeling the whole world (Pisces), thinking the whole world (Gemini) and shaping the whole world (Virgo).

Because of this diversity of orientation, these four people can only do what they want to do if they clearly distinguish between "I" and "you", if they separate themselves from each other, if they leave each other alone, if they are tolerant, if they take their freedom for themselves and leave their freedom for the others. These are exactly the qualities of an astrological square.

V 4.   The Twelve-Divided Circle

The twelve-divided circle seems to be the central element in all these considerations – and therefore probably also the source of the unified world view.

V 4. a)   The Zodiac, the Four Elements and the Three-Step

The circle, divided into twelve equal sections of 30° each, is found in its simplest form as the superstring and as the zodiac. From it the qualities of the angles can be derived, i.e. more exactly these angles with their qualities form a coherent system in the form of the zodiac.

The twelve elementary particles do not form a circle, but they also have the inner structure of the "4·3=12", i.e. the four elements, which occur in three sizes/dynamics.

The superstring is the smallest unit and the foundation of today's physics. The zodiac is the foundation of astrology and also of a part of magic. Via the dynamics of the 120° angle and the three-step dynamics contained in it, the chakra system and the Kabbalistic Tree of Life are also a part of the zodiac. The eleven-dimensional mathematical model of the superstring theory corresponds again exactly to the Kabbalistic Tree of Life – which in turn is based on the three-step, which also characterizes the zodiac.

V 4. b)   The Twelve-divided Circle and the Tube Model

The two most fundamental of the structures found so far in the world are (in this book), first, the twelve-divided circle and, second, the tube model. These two structures are closely connected and are in the end only two different aspects of the same model:

> The "inside = outside" approach has led to the description of the world as an extremely complex tube system in which there is an "inside" and an "outside" corresponding to consciousness and matter.

The consideration of the angles in the world has led to the discovery of the seven basic qualities corresponding to the angles 0°, 30°, 60°, 90°, 120°, 150° and 180°. These qualities correspond to the astrological properties of the aspects that have these angles. The chakra system and the Kabbalistic Tree of Life can be derived from the 120° angle (three-step). The I Ching and the Ifa Oracle can be derived from the 180° angle (complementary opposition).

The tube model is derived from the image of a super string ("swinging circle") moving through time. The tubes of the tube model are therefore all twelve-divided circles.

The twelve-divided circle is the "substance" and the basic "form" of the tube system.

Thus, the twelve-divided circle is the basic element. The tube system is the consideration of the entire world as a vast network consisting of these circle-elements moving through time.

V 4. c) "In the Beginning there was the Twelve ..."

Through the considerations in the first two sections of this chapter, a comprehensive model emerges, with which both the magical and the physical phenomena of the world can be summarized in one picture.

However, a consideration is still missing to it, why the twelve-divided circle actually stands so clearly in the center of our world.

The simplest explanation for it are probably the properties of the space-time which are necessary so that the space-time can exist:

- The world must have originated – without the big bang, without the creation it would not exist.
This corresponds to the quality of the conjunction (**0°**).

- The elementary particles can be understood as curvatures of the space-time (mountains, valleys). So there must be a stable form in which the space-time can bend, otherwise there could be no constant elementary particles – the world would be otherwise an empty space in which time would not cause any changes.
This corresponds to the quality of the square (**90°**).

- There must be movement in the world, otherwise nothing could happen – and there could also be nobody who could perceive this world.

This corresponds to the quality of the opposition (**180°**).

- But there must also be an organic coherence and an organic development and unfolding in the world, otherwise everything would always remain the same.
This corresponds to the quality of the trine (**120°**).

- There must also be the possibility of group formation, since otherwise all things in the world would remain individual and there could be no large, differentiated structures.
This corresponds to the quality of the sextile (**60°**).

- There must also be the possibility of further development to completely new states, because otherwise everything would "freeze" quite fast in a single form. Time itself also needs this possibility – after all it is the flow of further development.
This corresponds to the quality of the semisextile (**30°**).

- Finally, there must be the possibility of fundamental change, because otherwise everything could get stuck in one state at some point.
This corresponds to the quality of the quincunx (**150°**).

So the qualities of the seven angles are "the necessary qualities of the world" – and they are also "the seven qualities of life".

If these seven angle qualities are the necessary basis, then the space-time can bend only in a way which contains these seven qualities – it can bend consequently only as a twelve-divided circle and can form thereby independent particles which can exist for a long time. If our world would be different, then we would not exist and probably also nothing else in this world.

If only things can form from the space-time which are twelve-divided circles or more complex forms of such twelve-divided circles, then all existing things should be such twelve-divided circles in the innermost. It should not matter whether one looks at a thing from the outside or from the inside – one finds either twelve-divided zodiacs or twelve-divided superstrings ...

V 4. d)   Causality and Analogy in the Tube Model

The whole world is a tube system in the model considered here. The overall shape of this system is shaped by two factors: causality and analogies.

    1. causality appears in this model in a very simple way:

        - For one thing, no tube simply ends in nothingness, but always continues into the future – where it can, of course, transform.

        - On the other hand, tubes can meet, unite, separate – like the representations in the Feynman diagrams in physics, which show exactly these connections.
        Everything affects everything else …

The causality, thus the temporally endless continuation of the tubes is basically nothing else than the pictorial representation of the laws of conservation: Things can transform, but nothing ever gets lost or arises out of nothing.
The big bang is the temporal beginning also of the tube model. At that time at the very beginning there was only space-time. It was a unity. From this beginning point, which had an unimaginably big density and heat, all tubes start.

    2. The analogies should appear in the tube model as a symmetry. This symmetry should unfold kaleidoscopically.
    Both astrology and the use of analogies in magic show that these analogies can be extremely diverse.

Causality and analogies appear in the tube model as the temporal beginning of all tubes in a single point (big bang) from which they expand, differentiate and unfold kaleidoscopically in a symmetrical manner. The fundamental element of both causality and analogies is the twelve-divided circle: the superstring and the zodiac.

V 4. e)   Analogies in the Tube Model

Now, what do analogy relations look like in the tube model? Can they be described as an aspect of the tube system – just as superstring and zodiac can be illustrated as the circle-form of the tubes?
First of all, the analogies can be taken as a self-similarity of the total system: All things are ultimately made up of elementary particles that have the shape of a superstring – and all born beings and created things have a horoscope based on the zodiac.

Everything is shaped by the twelve-divided circle – both internally in consciousness (zodiac) and externally in matter (superstring).

The order of analogy obviously refers not only to the elementary particles, but to beings of the most different size – otherwise there would be no horoscope for humans, animals, companies, states etc..

One could assume that only analogies with one of the "seven qualities" are possible as "analogy essence", but this is not so, because one can also use e.g. the astrological planets, the tarot cards, the I Ching or the runes as analogy essence. So an analogy can not only have one of the seven angle qualities, but also others, which are partly much more manifold and complex. Of course, it is difficult to verify whether e.g. the tarot card "three of wands" is ultimately built up from these seven angle qualities.

The twelve-divided circle is found in physical terms first of all only on the very fundamental level as the superstring form of the elementary particles of which the object under consideration consists.

In a horoscope the zodiac appears as the basis of this horoscope which refers to the being as a whole.

The material body is the outside – it is determined. The consciousness is the inside – it is free. The transition between the two is what is usually called "life force" – it consists of qualities.

The twelve-part circle appears with the superstring in the matter, thus as quantity in the single elementary particle. With the horoscope it appears in the life force, thus as quality in the whole.

Here obviously two different levels of observation and order are present. The astrological level describes the physical level as a whole and can therefore make qualities, character traits and events clear.

This shows that the analogies must shape the form of the physical events in a comprehensive way – otherwise it would not be possible that astrology works so differentiated and continuously over thousands of years.

But how this order of analogies looks exactly in the tube model is still unclear for the time being.

V 4. f) Physics in the Tube Model

The physical conservation laws, the causality and the laws of nature are part of the tube model, because the form of the tube model is nothing else than the complex representation of the world as superstrings in the course of time. The tube model is merely the combination of the graphical representation of the superstrings as a twelve-part circle with the Feynman diagrams.

V 4. g)   Magic in the Tube Model

Magic has two aspects in the tube model – as it has in the concrete everyday life:

- On the one hand, there is consciousness, which shapes the world in a direct way by will and imagination: Telepathy, telekinesis and the like. In the tube model this is essentially an extension of the consciousness inside the tubes – the direct access to things outside the own body and also to the consciousness of other people, animals, plants and things.

- On the other hand, analogies are often used in magic, which can reduce the required amount of will and imagination. So, within the tube system there seem to be easy ways of expanding consciousness (with analogies) and difficult ways of expanding consciousness (without analogies).

To the magic effect of will and imagination also belongs the magic effect of wishes and fears as images (imaginations) in the consciousness – they also evoke analogies. A wish evokes the fulfillment of that wish and a fear evokes in the same way the experience of which one is afraid. In both cases, analogies spontaneously arise on the outside to the images on the inside.

One can now wonder how these analogies, which shape the tube system, look like as a whole.
Is the basic movement an equal behavior of all angular qualities in the world? This would correspond quite well to astrology, where the current planetary constellations affect all beings in the same way – whereby the respective way of reaction to this influence, which is the same for all, depends on the horoscope of the person concerned.
Is there therefore a "dance" which is the same for all elementary particles and which is based on the "choreography" which becomes visible through astrology?
However, this still does not describe in a vivid way the appearance of the analogy order in the tube model …

V 4. h)   Freedom, Analogy and Determinacy

An important point in this model is also the question of the connection between the determinacy of matter on the outside, the freedom of consciousness on the inside and the analogies in the area of the life force, thus at the transition between consciousness and matter. This life force area is the place which is essentially characterized by the twelve-divided circle.

- The determinacy of matter must have limits, because telepathy and telekinesis are possible. The determinacy of matter cannot be immovably fixed – there must be something like an "external inertia" of the world (and therefore of the tube system).

- The might of consciousness must have limits, because the world is not easily shaped just by will and imagination. The consciousness cannot easily become completely free – there must be something like an "internal inertia" of the consciousness (and therefore of the tube system).

Telepathy and telekinesis show that consciousness can also act directly on matter – not only on one's own body, but also on other bodies and likewise on the consciousness of other people and beings.

This expansion of the consciousness is in the tube model an expansion in the inside of the tube system beyond the border of the own body. This limit is not an obstacle in principle, but a threshold of inertia, beyond which one can go by will and imagination.

Matter has the inertia called "causality" – magic has the inertia called "idleness" and lack of vision, determination, will, concentration, imagination as well as lack of knowledge of the magic possibilities. It is through this inner inertia that the thresholds of consciousness arise.

In the end, both are the same inertia: Only when the consciousness, through its decisiveness, gains direct access to things outside of its own body, the physical laws are partially suspended and magic happens.

The life force as the transition between consciousness and matter is what is inert. It must be moved in magic. In doing so, one can make use of the properties of this life force, i.e. above all the qualities of the twelve-divided circle in the form of simple analogies, which one can use in imagination.

V 5.   The Analogies

In the previous considerations it has remained a little unclear in which way the analogies shape the world. It can be said that the world unfolds kaleidoscopically, but it would be quite welcome to know a little more about the patterns in this kaleidoscope. Since these patterns emerge through the analogies, it is useful to examine these analogies in more detail.

V 5. a)   Astrology

Zodiac and Aspects

The zodiac and aspects are universally valid analogies since they occur in astrology as well as in physics (superstring, angular qualities). Moreover, although there are many different astrological systems, the zodiac and the qualities of the aspects are the same in all of them.

The zodiac was created by naming the constellations in the sky and combining the sequence of constellations through which the sun, moon and planets pass into a sequence of twelve images. Initially, there were also sequences of ten or eleven constellations as the path of the planets in the sky.

However, the zodiac is calculated by the position of the earth to the sun. Since the earth's axis is oblique, there are the four seasons, which are separated by the longest night, the longest day and the two equinoxes in between. These four points in time mark the beginning of the four cardinal signs of the zodiac, i.e. Aries (spring equinox), Cancer (summer solstice), Libra (autumn equinox) and Capricorn (winter solstice).

So the zodiac is not up in the sky in the stars, but all around the earth. It is not the stars that send "rays" of astrological qualities to the earth, but it is the position of the earth in relation to the sun that determines the zodiac. Since the zodiac is therefore geocentric, the zodiac can be seen as an aura (="life force body") of the earth.

The interesting thing about this statement is that the elementary particles can be represented as super-strings, i.e. as twelve-divided circles – and that also the earth astrologically is surrounded by a twelve-divided circle, which can be recognized by means of the zodiac.

Strictly speaking, the earth rotates within this twelve-divided circle, whose position is determined by the position of the earth axis. This rotating of the earth in the twelve-divided zodiac is extremely similar to the conception of the superstrings as swinging, twelve-divided circles.

So it seems as if every system could be understood as a rotating twelve-part circle.

Possibly this is also true for the human being itself: There are twelve acupuncture meridians and the heart chakra as the center of the chakra system has twelve petals – although in older representations the heart chakra also appears with eight petals. However, since man is also "wrapped" in his horoscope, so to speak, it seems quite probable that man also has a twelve-part "aura".

The twelve-part circle is found therefore in the very small with the elementary particles, in the middle with the human being and in the very big with the zodiac of the earth.

One can assume therefore with some justification that all things in the world can be understood as twelve-divided circles – particularly since they all have their own horoscope and are therefore "zodiacal".

Thus the twelve-divided circle and the qualities of the seven angles in it would be a generally valid structure which is found with every independent thing – starting from a photon over animals, people, enterprises and states up to planets and presumably also suns and galaxies.

It would be useful to check whether the zodiac and astrology also exist if one leaves the earth – e.g. if someone is born on the moon, on Mars or on a planet orbiting the star Alpha Centauri. However, this is technically not feasible at the moment – and I have not yet thought of an experiment with which one could prove the existence of the zodiac e.g. for the planet Pluto or at least for the moon.

Planets

In astrology the planets are a logical sequence of properties:

- Moon	- perception	- infant
- Mercury	- thinking	- pupil
- Venus	- evaluate	- adolescent
- Sun	- deciding	- king
- Mars	- acting	- warrior
- Jupiter	- organize	- manager
- Saturn	- preserve	- guardian
- Uranus	- new	- inventor
- Neptune	- expansion	- artist
- Pluto	- essential	- magician

This logical sequence suggests at first that the planets are a universal system. However, this is not true for several reasons:

- One can include minor planets like Ceres and the like into this sequence, whereby it gets mixed up.

- In case of a birth on Mars, Mars would be missing as a planet in the horoscope of the person concerned. Would the person then have no muscles corresponding to Mars? In addition, the Earth would appear as a planet in the horoscope – what characteristics does it have then? Furthermore, the Earth Moon would disappear and the two Martian Moons would be added. Would a person born on Mercury not be able to think? And what happens with a birth on a spaceship which orbits the Jupiter which has after all 79 moons which would appear then also in the horoscope?

- In other solar systems there are the most different numbers of planets – and the possibly habitable planet must not always be the fourth of ten planets.

Now in astrology the planets have a logical sequence of qualities, which does not look arbitrary at all. Possibly all planetary sequences have such a logical sequence of qualities independent from which planet in which solar system one looks.

But at least one can say that not the planet in itself has a quality, but that e.g. Mars only seen from the earth has the quality of the warrior. On the other hand, seen from Mars as a birthplace, another planet will be responsible for muscles, work, sex and fight.

House system

The zodiac is based on the seasons, the house system is based on the times of day. The house system is like a second zodiac with similar characteristics, but with a different orientation. The zodiac signs each describe a style, the houses each describe an area of life.

Day and night have different lengths depending on the season and the place on earth, which is taken into account when calculating the houses. However, in the course of time different methods have been developed, in which the size of the individual houses can be different – each of these systems has evaluated the influence of the length of day and night on the size of the astrological houses differently.

Moreover, the usual house systems work only between the Northern Arctic Circle and the Southern Arctic Circle. This is because between the Arctic Circles and the poles there are times of the year when it is constantly night or constantly day. Then a division of the houses on the basis of the relationship between the length of the day and the length of the night is no longer possible.

The house system therefore does not seem to be such a universal system as the zodiac – although the house system works exceptionally well in the interpretation of horoscopes.

V 5. b) Systems of Analogy

There are many systems that divide the world into a group of elements that collectively represent all aspects of the world – each from the point of view of the system, of course. Each of these systems has a basic principle that has been used for the divisions in that system. Figuratively speaking, these systems sort the world according to different aspects: some divide things in the world according to their "color", others according to their "shape" and the third according to their "weight".

Thus, the 64-part I Ching and the 256-part Ifa Oracle use the complementary opposition (Yin and Yang) as a basic organizing principle. By this, these two systems describe the world as a constant change – this is the basic quality of the "2", i.e. the 180° angle, which is called "opposition" in astrology.

A very simple way to divide the world into similar areas is the four elements of fire, water, air and earth. Their basic principle is the energy level in which a thing is in the world: from the energy-rich fire to the less energy-rich air and the quite energy-poor water to the almost energy-less earth. The quintessence, that is the "fifth element" is just this energy itself, which the other four elements contain in varying degrees. Such a system always looks at the energy level of things.

The Kabbalistic Tree of Life, like the chakra system, uses the three-step as its basic principle – so it starts from the quality of the 120° angle. However, this principle has been further differentiated in the Tree of Life than in the chakra system. Consequently, the Tree of Life and the chakras consider the development of systems.

One can also use completely different systems as a basis for the division of the world, such as the Germanic gods in Asgard or the sweat lodge mandala with the four animals in the four directions, the earth below, the sky above and the secret of life ("wakan tanka") in the center.

The interesting point about these systems is that they work. One can structure all things in this world with the help of these systems, and one comes to helpful realizations. The most sophisticated of these systems is certainly the Kabbalistic Tree of Life.

Most of these systems are based on a basic principle, which is also found in the zodiac, like the complementary opposition of the 180° angle in the I Ching and the Ifa Oracle or like the three-step of the 120° angle in the chakra system and the Tree of Life. However, the functioning of such a system does not depend on whether its basic idea is based on one of the seven qualities represented by the angles in the twelve-divided circle.

The order of analogy in the world must be very profound and comprehensive if it is possible to divide the world in the most different ways and to obtain each time again meaningful systems of analogy.

V 5. c) Oracles

The basic idea in all oracles in which "pictorial aids" are used is that these aids as a whole represent all the elements of the world:

- The 18 or more runes represent all the themes that may be important in a person's life.

- The 64 hexagrams of the I Ching represent all the states that are possible in the world.

- The 78 cards of the Tarot represent all the stages of development that can occur in the world.

- The 256 gods of the Ifa oracle represent all the forces that exist in the world.

- The elements of a "bone oracle," which uses a collection of items that are meaningful to the oracle interpreter (e.g.: knife = danger; tooth = power; corn kernel = food; wolf hair = power animal), represent the elements of that oracle interpreter's world.

The sum of the elements of each oracle system is a reflection of the world. The mostly unspoken basic assumption of oracles is that a complete image of the world must always be in the same state as the world itself. As the functioning of such oracles shows, this analogy between the oracle elements and the world actually exists.

The remarkable thing is that these oracles always work – no matter how they are constructed. The essential point is only that they represent a picture of the world. This suggests that the analogical order of the world is so finely structured that one can look at it in any way and find "working analogies" every time.

V 5. d) Omens

With an oracle the initiative lies with the questioner and the execution with the oracle interpreter: I have a question and ask it to a seer, who then brings out her tarot cards, lets me draw a card and then interprets this card as an answer to my question.

With an omen, the initiative lies with the world and the interpretation with oneself or with an "expert". For example, if I am walking down the street with my head bowed, thinking about my poverty, and then suddenly a 50€ bill is lying in front of me on the road, this omen is not very hard to interpret …

However, there are also more complex omens, about which one must think for a while, but which give then also clearly more differentiated answers.

Finally, there are omens for whose interpretation a certain worldview is necessary – the omens usually refer to the worldview of the person to whom this omen refers.

It is difficult to decide whether an omen is a "conversation of the world with a person" or whether the person in question telepathically or telekinetically summons a certain omen. There are, of course, omens such as a landslide or news of the outbreak of a war in a particular country that one should take the precaution of not considering as telepathically/telekinetically caused by oneself.

Above all, the omens show that the order of analogy is not only present and visible when one asks a question of the world or uses an image of the world as an oracle (like the tarot cards), but that these analogies can also occur spontaneously.

In the end, astrology shows very clearly that the analogies work even if the person does not look for them – after all, every person has his horoscope that shapes him, no matter if he knows it, if he wants it, if he resists it or if he finds it extremely practical.

V 5. e) Omens, Oracles and Intuition

When one has questioned an oracle or interpreted an omen, one first receives a structure or a quality as an answer. One can classify a situation and guesses how it could develop further. However, all these answers remain first of all on the level of qualities such as "imminent danger", "self reflection is helpful", "imminent loss", "actions are beneficial", "it furthers one to cross the great water" etc.

When using e.g. several tarot cards as an answer to a question, these statements can become more differentiated, but they still remain descriptions of qualities.

However, one can switch from interpreting, for example, the tarot cards and describing the qualities shown by them to a direct perception, through which one can also telepathically make very concrete statements such as "You will meet an old friend tomorrow at 11:30am on a street in Bonn, whom you think is currently in Belgium."

The transition from the interpretation of omens and oracles to the direct perception of hidden or future things is a change into another mode of consciousness:

- In interpreting an omen or oracle, the mind looks at the tarot cards that have been drawn, for example, and interprets them using knowledge of those cards. This is an activity of the mind of the seer, who interpretes analogies.

- In intuition, the seer uses the tarot cards, the horoscope, the hexagrams of the I Ching, etc. as a "gateway" through which he then steps to see what he can perceive. This is an expansion of consciousness by the seer.

V 5. f) Analogies in Magic

In magic, analogies are used very frequently. Therefore, it is worth taking a closer look at what these analogies actually are in magic.

First of all, there is the analogy between the wish and the wish-fulfillment – or in other words between the will figuratively expressed by a ritual and the subsequent event. The magician wants to achieve something and for this he imagines the achieved as vividly and concentrated as possible. Of course, there are many different variants of this method, but the basic principle is that the alignment of the will and the imagination to the desired thing "pulls" this desired thing into one's own life. That this works, of course, can only be shown by one's own experience.

This principle works of course (unfortunately) also with a fear, on which one is fixed, and the "fear fulfillment" caused by it.

In general, one can say that emotionally charged images in the psyche tend to appear as events in the external world as well. This is a concrete application of the principle "inside = outside". If the consciousness is the inside of the world and matter is the outside of the world, then the images in the consciousness also shape the events in the person's life. The intensity of the events correspond thereby to the intensity of the feelings, which lie in these inner pictures. One could say instead of "feeling" and "emotions" also "charging with life-force".

In magic, it has been found that not only the imagined and "charged with life force" image, but the whole context of this image in the psyche is realized in the life of the person concerned. This is, if one starts from the principle "inside = outside", also not to be expected differently ...

The wish fulfillment is therefore rather an analogy to the total psyche than an analogy to the isolated wish which one has sent out. Ultimately, every "charged image" in the psyche also has an external effect.

So how important are analogies in magic?

In some rituals the analogies go very far, as for example in the so-called "Woodoo Magic", where a doll is made with the shape of the person you want to affect – preferably this doll also contains a hair or similar of the person concerned. If one wants to harm the person, this doll is pricked with needles – if one wants to heal the person, the doll is placed in the center in a ritual in which the gods are called to help.

In other rituals the analogies are, at least in part, simply aids in concentrating on a particular quality and in imagining that quality. For example, a red robe, a statue of Mars, holding a sword, a hematite cube on the altar, red candles, incense of nutmeg, etc., can promote inner alignment with Mars. Such a Mars ritual could be performed, for example, to become stronger, to have more sex, to win a fight, to cure a muscle ailment, etc.

The central element of such a ritual will quite certainly be the invocation of the god Mars. From experience, such invocations are quite effective – and consequently meaningful. But does the god Mars really exist? Is he a conscious being? Or is he a part of the world, i.e. a chain of analogies? Since one can divide the world according to the ten planets, the "Mars-tenth" of the world is really present. According to the principle "inside = outside" this "Mars tenth" of the world has also a consciousness, with which one can take up contact by concentration and imagination e.g. by a ritual and an invocation.

Of course, it remains unclear at first whether the "Mars tenth" is a natural unit of the world or whether this is a group of single elements created by human beings. The existence of the planet Mars in the sky and his meaning in astrology give to this "Mars tenth of the world" in any case already a great constancy – even if this quality cannot be traced back to one of the qualities of the zodiacal angles. But after all Mars is "related" to the zodiac signs Aries and Scorpio.

This consideration suggests that the analogies in magic are mainly concentration aids, imagination aids and aids in trusting one's own magic – even though the planet-gods seem to have a large measure of "natural reality".

The analogy systems in magic are very similar to the analogy systems used in oracles: They are man-made divisions of the world into certain basic qualities and basic dynamics. A concrete wish can be connected in magic to such a basic quality – of course to the quality which is most similar to the wish in question.

Since on the one hand oracles and magic work and on the other hand the analogy systems can be built up in many different ways, one can assume that the analogy structure of the world really exists, but that it can be viewed, ordered and systematized in different ways.

From this one can conclude that also the gods as the embodiment of basic qualities really exist. However, they exist presumably only as a continuum, whose division into

162

certain gods is to a large extent arbitrary. Seen in this way, the gods of the different peoples are all the same deity-continuum, so to speak the "god-level" of the world. The specific division of this continuum into particular gods is then a matter of the worldview and circumstances of the particular people who worship those gods.

Here again it is shown that the order of analogy does exist in the world, but that it is questionable whether there are "natural systems of analogy" which have not been created first by man as a division. As a "natural analogy system" the twelve-part circle and its seven angle qualities come after the previous considerations most likely into question.

However, this astrological-physical analogy structure is apparently so elastic and flexible that it can be viewed and ordered in the most diverse ways: through the Tarot, through the I Ching, through the Ifa Oracle, through the chakra system, through the Tree of Life, through the Runes, through the Greek Gods, through the Tibetan Mandalas, through the Four Elements, etc.

The fact that some of these systems are based on one of the seven angular qualities does not diminish the impressive flexibility of this universal analogical structure.

V 5. g) Miracles

One can, if one wishes, distinguish magic from miracles – or ordinary magic from extraordinary magic. Telepathy and the telekinetic moving of a paper-wheel as well as the magical summoning of a new dwelling would then be ordinary magic, while walking on water, lying unharmed on a carpet of embers, levitation, turning water into wine and the like would be extraordinary magic.

Several things are striking about the performance, witnessing and descriptions of such miracles:

1. Those who perform them are single-minded,
2. they trust completely in a deity or a "principle",
3. their will is relaxed, and
4. they make no or minimal use of analogies, imaginations, and rituals.

People who perform miracles, according to their descriptions, seem to be on another plane where everything is without delineations and where everything flows, where everything is a continuum, and where the contents of consciousness immediately translate into reality.

This is obviously the plane of the deities. On the Kabbalistic Tree of Life, this is the sphere Da'ath. Buddha calls this the "four limitless qualities of an enlightened one".

163

The people who perform a miracle certainly have a worldview, but they do not seem to use it in the form of an imagination or a ritual. They usually limit themselves to extremely simple words or gestures – for example, Christ merely said to the dead Lazarus, "Arise."

One has the impression that in miracles the extension of consciousness to that which is to be changed is far more important than the observance of analogies. The analogies exist, of course, as astrology, among others, shows, but they seem to be of only secondary importance for the performance of magic and miracles – although one should not underestimate the function of analogies as an aid to concentration and imagination.

The most compelling argument for this view of analogies comes from magic itself:

- One can perform rituals in which one uses a variety of correct analogies, but they have no effect due to the lack of determination, will, concentration, and vivid imagination.

- On the other hand, a short, determined gesture accompanied by a vivid imagination can have a great magical effect.

- In the end, the most effective form of magic is the spontaneously arising and at the same time relaxed conviction that exactly what one thinks is good will come. In this form of magic, which is also found in miracles, there is no doubt in the consciousness about the effectiveness of what one wants and what one does, i.e. there is no doubt that one will achieve what one wants.

It would seem, then, that both magic and miracles are ultimately nothing more than the overcoming of the inertia of consciousness and matter – which, of course, is ultimately the same thing. When this inertia has been overcome by concentration and imagination or, in an advanced stage of the magician, by conviction and relaxed serenity, what is in the consciousness translates spontaneously and without effort into reality. Then one can "move mountains".

The only problem is that this state is not so easy to achieve – or in other words: the inertia of consciousness and matter are not so easy to dissolve.

V 5. h) Quality, Analogy and Quantity

The life force (the transition from consciousness to matter) has clear qualities, but its quantity cannot be measured directly, even if the degree of concentration on a quality comes very close to a quantity.

In the material area there are clear quantities, from whose behavior the physical laws result.

In the realm of vital force, the like things behave in a like way – this is the principle of analogy. Probably the best known application of this principle today (besides the Woodoo dolls) is homeopathy, which proceeds according to the principle "like cures like" and which works in the realm of the life force. "Like" in this context means that two things have the same quality, that is, the same structure, the same dynamics, the same behavior.

Why do qualities appear in consciousness (and therefore also in the life force) and quantities in matter? The answer is simple: matter is measurable, because its units are delimited – consciousness is not delimited, which is why only qualities are recognizable there.

This principle is also found in Da'ath on the Tree of Life:

- No matter is found there anymore, but only energy. In contrast to the elementary particles, thus to the matter, energy quanta have no firm outer shell, i.e. they cannot collide with each other, but overlap (two light beams do not collide with each other).

- Da'ath is the realm of deities whose essence has two characteristics: they have a clear quality and they are boundless.

- When you come to Da'ath in meditation, you experience a very clear transition: You jump into a bottomless abyss and there is no longer any support or boundaries.

The experience of one's own individuality also changes fundamentally in Da'ath: One no longer defines oneself by a boundary to the outside ("matter principle"), but only by one's own quality ("energy principle").

This transition to Da'ath can be one of the most intense experiences in meditation.

This observation shows that when one approaches unity, that is, consciousness, one passes from delimited quantities to delimited qualities.

Quantities are the basis of causality – qualities are the basis of analogies.

V 5. i)   The Analogy Structure of the Tube Model

What can be said about the structure of the tube system which is characterized by analogies?

First of all, analogies are as fundamental a property of the world as causality: both are omnipresent and characterize all things, and they also work in the very small.

Causality can be summarized in many different formulas, ranging from the basic "$E = m \cdot c^2$" to the formation of table salt ($NaCl$) and the prescription of a remedy, to measures promoting the economy in a national economy. The basis of all these formulas always remains causality – no matter from which point of view one looks.

One can also divide the analogies into many different qualities, ranging from astrology to the Tree of Life to the runes. The basis of all these qualities always remains analogy – no matter from which system one looks.

The omnipresent effectiveness of causality is easy to understand – simply because we are used to it from everyday life and from our world view. It is easy to attribute the processes in the world to the processes between the atoms and finally to see as the basis of the world a complex mathematical-physical system of causal interactions.

The ubiquitous effectiveness of analogies are not so easy to grasp – simply because they are unfamiliar. But why shouldn't every elementary particle in the world have not only physical properties but also analogy qualities?

Just as the world as a whole develops causally, so it can also develop as a whole in analogies.

The natural forms of analogy are the zodiac and the aspects resulting from it, i.e. the seven angle qualities. This structure of twelve and these seven angular qualities are universal. They form the basis of the "analogy continuum" – just as the laws of nature form the basis of the "causality continuum".

Presumably everything has a twelve-divided "aura" which appears as the super-strings, as horoscopes, as the zodiac of the earth and so on.

Whether there is an order of analogy in the world going beyond the twelve-division of the circle and the seven angular qualities is doubtful – at least no clues for it have been found so far.

V 6. Time

Time is one of the four dimensions of space-time – in the simple representation form it belongs to the group "width, height, length, time"; in the complete form to the group "time, three extended space dimensions, six subatomic space dimensions, one summarizing space dimension", which is described by the superstring theory.

Time is therefore a part of the foundation of all existing things, since everything can be traced back to curvatures of space-time.

In physics anti-particles can also be understood as particles moving "backwards" in time, i.e. flying from the future into the past.

In magic it is shown that one can see into the future and remember past lives. Astrology clearly shows that the qualities of future points in time are already fixed today.

So it seems as if there is a fixed direction of flow for time from the past into the future, but as if at least the (sub-)consciousness could move away from the present into the future and into the past.

These "consciousness time journeys" are in the tube model movements of the consciousness in the inside of the tube system which is the representation of the world as twelve-divided circles which move through time. The possibility of "consciousness time travels" results already from the picture of the tube model.

Possibly the matter with the time is also more complex in the physics than one mostly assumes so far – the anti-particles could be a hint to this.

V 7.   Conservation Laws

In physics the conservation laws are one of the most important basics at all. They say that nothing can come into being out of nothing and that nothing simply disappears. Even more precisely formulated, one of these conservation laws reads as follows: "The sum of mass in a closed system remains the same." The same is true for energy, momentum, electric charge, color charge of quarks, spin (intrinsic rotation of elementary particles), etc.

Any fundamental property of elementary particles that cannot be transformed into another cannot become more or less in a closed system.

Therefore, the conservation law "The sum of mass in a closed system remains the same." is not quite true, but is, strictly speaking, "The sum of mass and energy in a closed system remains the same." This is because energy can turn into mass and vice versa ("$E = m \cdot c^2$").

Where is this principle of conservation laws found in magic or astrology? Also in magic there is no effect without cause – but this is rather an analogy to causality than to the conservation laws (even if causality can be derived from the conservation laws).

In astrology we find the fixedness of the time-qualities – but also this is rather a hint to the basic properties of time and causality (which is the temporal development of situations) than a hint to conservation laws.

Should the conservation laws exist only in physics, since physics describes the material world, which is completely determined?

Do the conservation laws not exist in magic and astrology because the consciousness is free? Or do they not exist there simply because magic and astrology do not consider quantities but qualities? Qualities have no quantities and consequently cannot be examined whether their quantities remain the same …

Is there something in magic and astrology which corresponds to the conservation laws? This could be most likely the preservation of the analogy structure:

> - As physics considers quantities, it finds the conservation laws relating to quantities (amounts) – the conservation of the quantities of mass/energy, momentum, electric charge, color charge, spin, etc.

> - As magic considers qualities, it finds the conservation laws that relate to the qualities (analogies) – the conservation of the order of the analogies of the zodiac and the seven angle qualities.

V 8.   General Principles

Now one can still look whether there are statements within the tube model, which summarizes the physical and the magic world view, which apply in both world views. These would be then not only physical formulas or magic analogies, but more general statements, which apply both in physics and in magic – so to speak "magical-physical principles".

These following statements are, of course, only first contours and sketches, i.e. attempts to grasp the "basic framework" of the tube model.

1. **unity and multiplicity**: The world is a unity at its root, which has a differentiated form in its crown.

2. **inside and outside**: The inside (consciousness) corresponds to the outside (matter). Inside acts on inside, inside acts on outside, outside acts on inside and outside acts on outside. Inside and outside are equally real and equally effective.

3. **causality and analogy**: The world is equally ordered by causality and by analogy.

4. **conservation laws**:   The quantity (amounts) and quality (analogies) of all things in the world are conserved: Nothing comes from nothing; Nothing goes to nothing.

5. **cause and effect**: Causes have an effect; effects have a cause. This applies to both quantitative changes (physics) and qualitative changes (magic, astrology).

6. **The twelve-divided circle**: All systems have the basic structure of a twelve-divided circle, which includes the seven angular qualities. The twelvefold circle is the zodiac on the inside and the superstring on the outside.

7. **unfoldment**: All systems unfold and develop according to the "three-step", which in its coarse structure resembles the chakra system and the surrounding space of the sun, and in its differentiated structure corresponds to the Kabbalistic Tree of Life.

8. **change**: The emphasis of an element in a pattern changes the pattern – no matter whether the emphasis is caused by the physical change of a quantity or by the magical emphasis of a quality.

169

9. **inertia**: The relative constancy and predictability of the world is due to the inertia of matter and consciousness. The more mobile and one-directed and thus also less inert the consciousness is, the less is also the matter inert – then the consciousness can form the matter increasingly freely: magic and miracles …

V 9.   Causality, Analogy and Magic

There seem to be at least three basic structures or dynamics in the world by which the forms, processes and possibilities in it are shaped: causality, analogy and magic. It might be helpful, therefore, to look a little more closely at the precise relationship between these three principles.

V 9. a)   Causality

Of the above three principles, causality is the easiest to describe, since our present civilization is based almost exclusively on this principle.

Every cause has an effect that results completely from those causes. Consequently, if one knows a situation completely in every detail, one can accurately predict the future development of that situation. On this principle is based, for example, the possibility of sending space probes from Earth to Pluto and taking pictures of Pluto, studying its atmosphere, measuring its magnetic field, and so on.

Thereby the development is considered in the temporal course. The description of this course is based in the core on physics, whose formulas are again the mathematical formulation of the conservation laws. These conservation laws simply state that nothing can disappear or come into being out of nothing. From this then a certain behavior of matter and energy results. In this world view everything is completely determined.

The non-determined phenomena like the only statistically determined decay of particles or the virtual particles are found only in the subatomic area. There the considered particles are so small that they do not behave any more exclusively like small spheres – in this area of the tiny sizes it shows up that all particles are actually curvatures of the space-time and have therefore no sharp borders, but are " hills that are flattened at the edge" in the space-time.

However, these non-determined phenomena in the subatomic realm have no effect on the fact that in our everyday life with its "normal quantities" all things behave in a determined way, i.e. develop in a predictable way.

V 9. b) Analogy

The existence of analogies can be shown in two ways without much effort: on the one hand by astrology and on the other hand by analogy systems like the cabbalistic tree of life.

However, a closer look shows that there are different types of analogies that appear in different contexts:

1. physical formulas: Through observation of nature, increasingly accurate descriptions of the processes within it have emerged over time.

Through the exact measuring finally the physical formulas could be formulated like e.g. "force = mass · acceleration" or "momentum = mass · velocity". These formulas show that the same processes always develop in the same way: These processes behave analogous to each other. Seen in this way, the physical formulas are "quantitative analogies".

These analogies, thus the physical formulas, show that the material world is a unit, whose parts behave everywhere in the same way. Thus, on a fundamental level, the world is an organic unity.

2. astrology: astrology also originated from the observation of nature – only here not quantities and sizes were considered, but qualities and intensities.

This has shown that the events in the world do not only follow the rules of causality, but that they also have a common rhythm – the events in this world perform a common dance.

It is possible to calculate a horoscope for all beings and things, which describes the character and lifestyle of these beings and things. By comparing the horoscope of a person, for example, with the position of the planets at a certain moment, it is also possible to describe the current state of that person. Astrology is therefore an all-encompassing principle of order.

Finally, with the help of astrology it is possible to calculate events and developments that are still in the distant future.

This form of analogies, like the totality of the formulas of physics, exists already in the world and has not to be created by man – it can be observed and described by man.

3. oracle: Here the situation is a little different. One can use the most different systems to receive an answer to the question about the quality of a moment or about the prospective development of a situation. For this purpose one uses tarot cards, the I Ching, the runes or any other system whose parts represent a complete picture of the world.

Strictly speaking, however, the difference between astrology and, for example, the tarot is not as great as it seems at first sight. The difference is mainly that astrology uses a system that already exists independently of the human being (the position of the planets) in order to arrive at statements about the current quality – while, for example, with the Tarot, a system (the Tarot cards) had to be created first in order to arrive at these statements.

In astrology one observes a part of the world (the planets), in order to conclude then with the help of analogies on the condition of all parts in this world (e.g. as Horoskop), while with the Tarot one uses a man-created system, in order to develop from it the answer to the posed question as analogy to the cards drawn "by coincidence". The drawing of the cards matching the question is of course no coincidence, but the analogy between the tarot cards as a picture of the world and the world itself.

4. omens: With omens the situation is again somewhat different than with astrology (one always looks at the planets) and with the oracles (one always looks at a "picture of the world"). In observing omens, one is simply attentive to things that are happening that are in some way striking.

This can be the conspicuous flight of a bird, or a brief encounter in which you are told something helpful by someone you don't know, or more complex events such as three arrows that you suddenly discover in front of you in the meadow you are walking across, and whose condition and arrangement gives you the answer to the question about your relationship with a couple you are friends with and have just been thinking about intensely.

With an omen there is no permanent system like in astrology and also no system created and selected by people like the I Ching, but so to speak a "spontaneous system" which shows up in this special situation as an analogy to what has just occupied one intensively. Strictly speaking, omens are not a system, but the spontaneous appearance of an analogy and the comprehension of this analogy.

In the beginning there is one's own intensive occupation with a subject. This topic in one's own psyche, charged with intense feelings, then evokes an analogy to this topic and all its facets in the outside world in the form of a striking event. Since this omen, i.e. the conspicuous event, reflects not only the subject's question but his entire situation, this omen can be experienced as an answer to the subject's question.

The omen is an analogy to the whole inner state of a person in relation to a certain subject. Therefore, the omen as a reflection of this inner totality can help this person to recognize himself and thereby find an answer to the question about his subject.

5. <u>ordering principles</u>: The Kabbalistic Tree of Life, the I Ching, the Mandalas and similar systems show that there are many forms of analogies in the world, which can be represented as different systems. All these systems work equally everywhere.

These systems can be based like the Tree of Life on the three-step, or like the I Ching on the complementary opposition or like the Mandalas on the combination of different principles. (In mandalas, these are usually the "4" of the elements and the "3" of development.)

However, as the oracle systems show, the world can be structured not only with the help of analogy systems derived from one of the qualities of the zodiacal angles, but also from relatively arbitrary systems like the sequence of runes.

6. <u>General order of analogy</u>: Astrology, oracles and omens show that there is a general order of analogy in the world, which can be grasped in many ways.

While the physical formulas are "quantity analogies", the analogies in magic and astrology are "quality analogies".

7. <u>desire and effect</u>: Still another form of the analogy is the connection between desire and effect and/or between fear and effect: The feeling in the inside calls the event in the outside, which fits to it.

This principle is used in magic, but it is also the basis of omens, in which an event or situation spontaneously occurs on the outside that corresponds to the emotionally charged theme on the inside. The omen allows the structures and dynamics in that theme to become clearer.

Ultimately, there are two basic forms in this variety of analogies:

1. There is a general order of analogies in the outside, which can be perceived with the help of astrology and oracles (quality analogies) and which is also the basis of the formulas of physics (quantity analogies).

2. There are "magic analogies", by which an intense inner state, usually connected with an inner image, causes a corresponding outer event – that is, an analogy between inside and outside, that is, between consciousness and matter.

If this happens spontaneously, this is either an omen or a spontaneous wish fulfillment; if this happens intentionally with the help of "will and imagination", this is magic.

However, both forms of analogy can be understood as two sides of a basic analogy order in the world:

- The general analogies become visible through the observation of the world;

- the magical analogies become visible through the individual magical action.

If the analogy-order is as much a fundamental feature of the world as causality, it should also be able to appear in these two ways – i.e. in connection with the ability to perceive and in connection with the ability to act.

The pair "ability to perceive and ability to act" is of course again a distinction from the point of view of causality, which considers the temporal developments – from the magical point of view one can simply say that an event is in analogy to a human being (and his perceptions and actions).

This general order of analogy causes that

"like affects like",
"like causes like",
"like acts on like",
"like develops like",
"everything has the same structure"
  etc.

This basic order of analogy obviously has several properties:

1. It is all-encompassing. It structures the entire world.

2. It can be viewed in many different ways. It can be described with the help of astrology and also with the help of the Tarot, the Tree of Life, the Chakras, the Runes, the I Ching, the Bach Flowers, the Ifa Oracle, the Omens, etc. There is not only one order of analogy, but a variety of possible orders of analogy – the order of analogy is a basic property of the world like causality.

This means that the order of analogy is, so to speak, "plastic", that it has no "form in itself" excluding other forms, that it can be viewed from the most diverse directions and points of view, and that it can, so to speak, take on an infinite number of shapes.

3. The analogy is like the causality also an effect connection. This can be seen, among other things, in magic, in omens and in homeopathy, all of which are based on an action of analogies.

The analogies in the world are thus 1st all-embracing, 2nd "formless-plastic" and 3rd effective.

The natural form of analogies is found in the twelve-part circle with its seven angular qualities.

V 9. c) Magic

One can understand magic as an effective analogy between two things: between the contents of the consciousness charged with the help of emotions or concentration in the inside and the events corresponding to these contents in the outside.

However, magic can also be seen as an expansion of consciousness in which the consciousness, that is, the will and imagination of the magician, expands to beings and things in the world and shapes and directs events in the world according to one's wishes.

In the case of making a talisman to help in finding a suitable home, the description with the help of the analogy model is obvious at first. But one can regard this process also as an extension of the consciousness of the magician on exactly this suitable dwelling.

With hypnosis, telepathy and telekinesis one will think first of all of an extension of the consciousness to other people, beings and things, but also here one could describe these processes as an analogy between the magician and that, on which he influences or about which he gets to know something.

In homeopathy, an analogy is created between the patient and the substance from which the globule has been made, by taking the globule. But one could also say that the consciousness of the globule substance is extended to the patient.

If two things (like here the analogy-effect and the consciousness-extension) cannot be distinguished, they must be the same in the end. Only what can be distinguished can be different.

This argumentation was also used by Albert Einstein during the development of his theory of relativity: There are situations in which gravity cannot be distinguished from centrifugal force – consequently both must be the same force.

So one can join Einstein here and say that the analogies and the expansion of consciousness must be the same, because in magic one cannot distinguish between them.

Of course, the question arises what this equality of analogy-effect and conscious-ness-expansion means.

With regard to magic it is known that all things first develop causally – as long as the consciousness does not interfere and cause a magic effect. Matter is therefore not completely causally determined, but only inert, whereby it behaves within the normal determinacy (causality) and according to the conservation laws in a predictable way.

The consciousness also has this inertia and tends to get stuck in its rut. However, it can also concentrate and thereby expand its range of perception and action and then finally produce a magical effect. This expansion of the consciousness can be understood just as well as the activating of analogies.

Thus, both in matter and in consciousness there is an inertia which is closely connected with causality and determinacy. However, this inertia can be overcome by consciousness – wherein ultimately the freedom of consciousness is shown.

If the consciousness tries to overcome the inertia of matter and to become magically effective through it, it concentrates on an image, a feeling or the like, thus on a quality. The consciousness thus becomes active in the realm of qualities – which is often experienced and described as "directing the life force".

The concentration on a certain quality in the inside calls for the same quality in the outside. Thus, a purposeful analogy is created between the inner and the outer. When this analogy arises in the outside to the "charged with life force" image in the inside, one can also say that the consciousness of the person concerned has extended to this analogy in the outside.

So there is no difference between the analogy activation and the consciousness expansion:

      - The description of overcoming the inertia of consciousness (con-centration) and matter (magical effect) as "analogy activation" considers the process from the emergence of an analogy.

      - The description of overcoming the inertia of consciousness (con-centration) and matter (magic effect) as "consciousness-expansion" considers the process from the activity of consciousness.

Consciousness moves in qualities – which automatically leads to a description of the processes of consciousness characterized by analogies, because the contents of consciousness consist of qualities with certain intensities. Thus, in magic, the consciousness constantly acts in the realm of analogies – the analogies are the map of qualities in which the consciousness of the magician wanders and acts.

So the principle of analogy-ordering and the principle of "inside = outside" are ultimately the same principle describing the qualities-side of the world – as opposed to physics, which describes the quantities-side of the world.

C A New View

Now that at least a first sketch of the unified world view has been formulated, one can also look at what effects this sketch could have on the current world view or where there are points of connection of this model to the current world view.

VI The Overall Picture

The tube model is the sketch of an overall picture of the world, in which among other things the consciousness and the matter appear equally.

Consciousness is the inside of the world – matter is the outside of the world. Both affect each other: matter on matter, matter on consciousness, consciousness on matter (including telekinesis) and consciousness on consciousness (including telepathy).

   - The matter side of the world is described by quantities, the consideration of which leads to the recognition of the conservation laws and causality.

   - The consciousness side of the world is described by qualities, the consideration of which leads to the recognition of the preservation of the analogy order and to the recognition of the analogy effect, which is an extension of the consciousness.

The tube model describes the world as a "differentiated unity":

   - The "inner side" of this model is the fundamental unity (matter: spacetime; consciousness: "God").

   - The "outer side" of this model is the multiplicity of appearances (matter: particles; consciousness: analogies).

   The simultaneous effect of the quantity laws (causality) and the quality laws (analogies) leads to a kaleidoscope-like unfolding of the world.

The inertia of matter lets the world appear constantly and exclusively causal.
The inertia of consciousness makes the consciousness appear delimited – this inertia

179

creates the thresholds of consciousness, which can be dissolved by a sufficient concentration.

VII The "Parent Epoch"

It is no coincidence that this book is written just in the year 2021. It belongs to a large number of similar processes, which all have the same quality and orientation and are therefore analogies to each other.

Many of them work rather unnoticed on a small scale, but some of them also on a large scale like the following things:

- the founding of the UN after the Second World War as a coordination system of states, whose main task is to prevent wars;

- the closely related disarmament efforts, made urgently necessary by the possibility of mankind's self-destruction through its atomic bombs;

- the protection of the environment, including the reduction of global warming, the avoidance of waste and the purely biological production of foodstuffs;

- the slowing down of overpopulation;

- ending famine;

- ending the extinction of species;

- etc.

All these initiatives on a large and political scale, as well as the many initiatives on a small and private scale, look at the whole and aim at the preservation of humanity as a species on this planet. They see humanity as a whole and not just the individual human being or the individual state.

The realization that one cannot completely separate oneself from the others on earth, but that mankind is one all-embracing system, corresponds to the lack of boundaries ("Da'ath"), which has already been described several times in this book and which is also one of the basic characteristics of consciousness.

Therefore it is not surprising if in this epoch, which began approximately in the 20 years after the Second World War, there is also a striving for a comprehensive, unified world view. The present book is a part of this effort.

VII 1.   The Seven Epochs

The new epoch that began about 65 years ago can be better understood by looking at the overall development, that is, by taking a closer look at the different epochs that have existed so far.

These epochs also correspond to the developmental phases in the life of an individual.[11]

VII 1. a)   Paleolithic Age

In the Paleolithic Age, people lived together in families that numbered about a dozen. One lived as part of nature in nature and was completely in the here and now.

The equivalent in the biography is the oral phase, in which the baby accepts everything, i.e. puts into its mouth, what is handed to it.

This phase is characterized by a simple, comprehensive and undifferentiated "Yes".

Therefore, one orients oneself to the contacts with the other people of one's own clan – "to those who are there".

Accordingly, the world is simply sorted by associations – what one has experienced with someone shapes one's relationship to that person. The basic distinction is the question "How close?" The mental basis of actions is the principle "contact forms connection."

This contact is also experienced as an exchange of "life force", so that touch is also an essential part of healing, soothing, protection and many other things – "contact magic". This life force contact is also possible with animals and plants. In such a world view telepathy is something normal, because "contact creates connection".

The experiences and views are expressed by pictures (cave paintings, statuettes, totem poles, etc.).

The support lies in the parents and later after their death in the ancestors, thus in the parents in the beyond.

---

11 A more detailed description may be found in my book „Die sieben Schritte des Lebens".

VII 1. b)   Neolithic Age

In this epoch, people lived together in clans that grew into small villages. Life as part of nature was now replaced by the opposition of field/pasture and wilderness, i.e. a struggle of culture against nature.

This corresponds to the "No!" of the infant in the anal phase, in which it also lives in the opposition of what it wants and what it does not want.

The orientation in the now clearly more complex world is reached by comparisons, i.e. by analogies, whose essential elements are the myths. Time is no longer the boundless present in the here and now as in the Paleolithic, but the cycle, which is, so to speak, the temporal aspect of the analogies: every year is analogous to every other year.

The logic of the analogy affects also to the way of acting, which is used in healings, in agriculture and many other things: "like affects like". On a grand scale, this is the cult that invokes the desired by displaying it (e.g., a good harvest). The basis for the cult are the myths, i.e. the essence of the entire analogies of a culture.

The backing is now no longer found in the parents/ancestors, but primarily in the gods, who are the "active essences" of the myths. Historically, the gods have developed for the most part from the ancestors. However, one found security not only in the gods themselves, but also in the myths, since they showed "how things are" and what one could rely on.

In this world view, one was not only connected with the people of one's own family, but above all with one or more of the deities under whose protection one placed oneself – as shown, among other things, by the many personal names which consist of a god's name and a gift of this deity (e.g.: ancient Egyptian "Sethnacht" = "strength of the god Seth" or Germanic "Thorfast" = "steadfastness of the god Thor").

VII 1. c)   Kingship

In this epoch people lived together as a nation defined as "inhabitants of a kingdom ruled by a king".

In individual development, this epoch corresponds to the phallic phase, in which the child discovers the "I!!!" that obviously corresponds to the king.

Both the king and the I are centerings. From this center all power emanates. Therefore, the whole (people, psyche) is structured and directed by the will of this centre (king, I) with the help of the principles (law, resolution) established by it. In this epoch the bigger numbers (more than a dozen), the writing and the form are invented in order to be able to grasp the multiplicity of the whole statistically and to be able to steer the people thereby better.

This centralism is also found in logic. The association of the Paleolithic and the analogy of the Neolithic are now followed by philosophy: From a First Cause (which corresponds to the will of the king and the I) the structure and the behavior of the whole (people, psyche) is derived. The whole (people, psyche) finds its support in the center: the psyche in the I, the community in the king, the religion in the One and Only God and the philosophy in the First Cause.

The will of the "One in the center" (God, King, I) is the measure of all things.

In the world view, therefore, God and man, will and instincts, king and subject, eternity and transitoriness, law and crime, virtue and sin, etc. are opposed to each other: "I" and "not-I".

Accordingly, support is sought from God (monotheism), from the king (loyalty) and from one's own ego (world view of Buddha, Lao-tse, Konfu-tse, Jaina, Zarathustra, Pythagoras, etc.).

The essential maxim of behavior is "through identification arises consubstantiality".

On this is based the loyalty to the king, the integration of the psyche, the mystical unity with God and also the magic of this epoch, which always begins with the identification with a deity ("invocation").

The contents of this epoch are formulated as divine revelation, royal law, and human self-knowledge. All three have in common the derivation from one basic principle, which means that they are three variants of philosophy.

VII 1. d)   Materialism

In this epoch different peoples live together, fight against each other, make alliances and break them again.

In biography, this is the genital phase, i.e. puberty. The individual tests his strength and his possibilities, conquers a place in the world and searches for a partner of the opposite sex. This exploration of the world is ultimately a question presented with courage: "You?"

Time is now seen for the first time as exclusively linear – in the Paleolithic it was the present, in the Neolithic it was a cycle, and in kingship time was the eternity of unity (God) and the transience of multiplicity (the world).

According to linear time, causal connections are analyzed, which first gave rise to the sciences, and as a result of them, technology and industrialization – power over the world. The way in which the world is represented is essentially mathematics.

Through the linear and purely materialistic view of this epoch, the consciousness of man is conceived as isolated from everything for the first time in its long history. This results in an existentialist contradiction between the individual and the world. Consequently, the support lies only in one's own strength – a struggle for survival characterized by the right of the strongest.

VII 1. e) New Epoch

In this epoch, which began around 1960, people experience humanity as a whole as their community.

This corresponds to the adult phase, i.e., the adult who takes care of his whole family – he rests in confidence in the whole and bears responsibility for the whole: "We."

People think in systems and look at overall contexts and look for "what works" – and for the whole. Within this worldview, time is a continuum in which one includes past, present and future equally in one's considerations and actions. One of the most important concepts (and impulses) is integration, because only through it can the multiplicity become a functioning whole that promotes all.

One's own identity is experienced as an aspect of the whole – one is part of the whole and connected to everything. One lives in trust because one is carried by the whole – and one lives in responsibility because one carries the whole.

The essence of this worldview is "Everything affects Everything".

VII 1. f) Summary of the Five Epochs

The characteristics of these five epochs have been summarized again in the following table:

Characteristics of the five epochs					
Characte-ristics	**the five epochs**				
	Paleolithic	*Neolithic*	*Kingship*	*Materialism*	*New epoch*
community	family	clan	people	peoples	mankind
orientation	in nature	culture - wilder-ness	own - foreign	feasibility	preservation
age	baby	infant	child	youth	adult
biography correspon-dence	oral phase	anal phase	phallic phase	genital phase	adult phase
essence	Yes	No!	Me!!!	You?	We.
conside-ration of:	contact	simile	identities	spatiotemporal developments	systems
logic	association	analogy	philosophy	science	functionality
method	how close?	compa-rison	centering	analysis	integration
principle	"contact forms connection"	"like acts on like"	"identification creates equality of essence"	"causality"	"everything affects everything"
time	present	cycles	eternity of unity - transitoriness of multiplicity	linear time	space-time continuum
representa-tion	image	analogy	principle	mathematics	overall representation
practical application	life force magic	analogy-magic	mysticism	technology and industry	preservation of mankind
support	parents/ancestors	gods	God	causality	humanity/world
	basic trust, perception	sheltered in myths	resting in God	to affirm existentialist contradiction	being part of the whole: trust and responsibility
expanding conscious-ness to:	human/animal/plant	deities	God	the consciousness of the individual is isolated	mankind/world

VII 1. g)   Future

It is foreseeable that there will be two more epochs in the future:

- The first of them corresponds to the older person, whose children have grown up and who now gets to know new things, undertakes journeys, pursues his hobbies and teaches others his experiences and knowledge. This is the "tutorial phase".
Here a greater freedom emerges.
This phase can be summarized as "Other …".

- The second future phase corresponds to the old man who retires, who appreciates silence and nature, and who has become wise. He recognizes the finiteness of his life and can be of great help to others. This is the "gerontic phase".
Here arises the realization of unity, out of which arises multiplicity.
This phase can be summarized as "All"

The seven phases have a clear inner logic, which can be divided into three developmental steps:

- baby: "Yes"
- infant: "No!"
- child: "I!!!"

- child: "I!!!"
- youth: "You?"
- adult: "We."

- adult: "We."
- older person: "Other …"
- old person: "All"

At the moment mankind is at the beginning of growing up after its materialism-puberty – which is not an easy time in the development of an individual human being, as experience shows …

VII 2. The 5th Epoch

The epoch at the beginning of which we find ourselves today is an analogy to the coming of age of the individual, which includes founding a family and looking at the whole. It is the epoch of parenthood.

This attitude is characterized by trust and responsibility: being carried by the whole in trust and carrying the whole in responsibility.

Looking at the whole also requires a new "story" that describes life as a whole in this era:

> - The narrative of the struggle of the good (= I, we, God) against the bad (= the other, the others, devil) no longer works if all are part of a whole – this story would only destroy humanity. These stories usually end with the victory of the good and the death of the evil.

> - Instead, a story is needed that focuses on the pursuit of the well-being of humanity as a whole. In this story, all are parts of a whole. Therefore, it is no longer about the struggle against the evil ones, but about the search for a behavior and an agreement with which all can live together. This then becomes the story of an "evolution of the system".

On the tree of life, this epoch corresponds to Da'ath, that is, to the principle of the absence of boundaries, already mentioned several times.[12]

It is quite probable that in this epoch the gods will again play a greater role, since they represent basic principles and are images that are unambiguous in quality and boundless in extent and therefore correspond to Da'ath.

One can assume that in this epoch magic and religion will be integrated together with the natural sciences to a uniform, comprehensive world view. This also means, among other things, that consciousness and matter will be regarded as equal and equally real components of the world – this is the main point considered in this book.

Therefore also magic in its many variants will very probably become again a component of the general world view. Approaches to this can already be found in positive thinking, in homeopathy, in Bach flowers, in the renaissance of astrology, in the increased interest in yoga and the most diverse religions and wisdom teachings, and finally also quite concretely in the constantly growing interest in telepathy, telekinesis and magic in general.

---

12 from primates to humans = Malkuth; paleolithic = Yesod; neolithic = Hod/Netzach; kingdom = Tiphareth; materialism = Geburah/Chesed; new epoch = Da'ath; future 1 = Binah/Chokmah; future 2 = Kether.
A more detailed description may be found in my book „Die sieben Schritte des Lebens".

VII 3.   New Ways of Behavior

In the meantime there are even sayings like "the world is a village" or guiding principles like "think globally, act locally", which show that the new view of the "parents of the earth" is gradually taking shape.

The increased interest in alternative ways of life, in ancient cultures, in the most diverse religious systems also makes it clear that a new view is currently emerging in the form of a grassroots revolution, i.e. that a great many small pieces of the puzzle are being discovered by a great many people, which are then being put together to form a complex, new world view. This happens mostly in everyday life and not in academic discourse – but with the various "green" parties this way of thinking has long since reached politics and in some cases even teaching in schools. Family constellations are also a magical method – they are a complex form of telepathy that originates from African ancestor cults.

The combination of magic and causality has not progressed too far yet, but at least telepathy, telekinesis, astrology, oracles, meditation, magic and the like have become more and more socially acceptable – around 1965 you had to search for a long time to find someone who even knew what the word "telepathy" meant.

Presumably, magic will gradually become a normal method of dealing with every-day problems: to investigate the cause of an illness and cure it, to find a suitable apartment, to find a lost key again, to increase one's circle of friends, to experience sexuality more intensively, to be able to understand one's own lifestyle better with the help of one's own horoscope, to be able to evoke the groundless inner joy, to get to know one's own soul and thereby understand oneself and one's own life theme, to recognize one's own power animal and one's own power plant and one's own power stone and thereby be able to consciously ask these three allies for help … the list of possible applications is almost endless …

English Books by Harry Eilenstein

- Living Magic (261 S.)
- The Synthesis of Physics and Magic (192 S.)

The following books will be published soon:

- Telepathy for Beginners
- Telepathy for Advanced Learners
- Telekinesis for Beginners
- Life Force for Beginners
- Meditation for Beginners
- Kundalini for Beginners
- Hypnosis for Beginners
- Auto-Movement for Beginners
- Chakra-Magic for Beginners
- Astral Projection for Beginners
- Astrology for Beginners
- Ritual Magic for Beginners
- Mandalas for Beginners
- Money Magic for Beginners
- Love Magic for Beginners
- Invocations for Beginners
- Evocations for Beginners
- Elves for Beginners
- Magic Research for Beginners
- Self-awareness for Beginners
- Symbolism of Numbers for Beginners
- Language of the Moon – for Beginners
- Magic Chant for Beginners
- Prophecy for Beginners
- Schamanism for Beginners
- Magic Objects for Beginners
- Da'ath-Magic for Beginners
- Crop Circles for Beginners
- Feng Shui for Beginners
- Magic for Beginners – Collection I
- Magic for Beginners – Collection II
- Magic for Beginners – Collection III

Bücher von Harry Eilenstein

Religion allgemein
- Die sieben Schritte des Lebens (428 S.)
- Muttergöttin und Schamanen (168 S.)
- Göbekli Tepe (472 S.)
- Die Göttin von Göbekli Tepe (144 S.)
- Totempfähle (440 S.)
- Christus (60 S.)
- Dakini (80 S.)
- Vajra (76 S.)

Ägypten
- Hathor und Re 1: Götter und Mythen im Alten Ägypten (432 S.)
- Hathor und Re 2: Die altägyptische Religion – Ursprünge, Kult und Magie (396 S.)
- Isis (508 S.)

Indogermanen
- Die Entwicklung der indogermanischen Religionen (700 S.)
- Wurzeln und Zweige der indogermanischen Religion (224 S.)

Germanen
- Die Götter der Germanen (87 Bände – siehe nächste Seite)
- Odin (300 S.)

Kelten
- Cernunnos (690 S.)
- Taliesin (228 S.)
- Der Kessel von Gundestrup (220 S.)
- Der Chiemsee-Kessel (76)

Psychologie
- Über die Freude (100 S.)
- Das Geheimnis des inneren Friedens (252 S.)
- Das Beziehungsmandala (52 S.)
- Gefühle und ihre Verwandlungen (404 S.)
- einsgerichtet (140 S.)
- Liebe und Eigenständigkeit (216 S.)
- Von innerer Fülle zu äußerem Gedeihen (52 S.)

Heilung
- Die Symbolik der Krankheiten (76 S.)

Kunst
- Herz des Tanzes – Tanz des Herzens (160 S.)

Drama
- König Athelstan (104 S.)

Bücher von Harry Eilenstein

„Magie für Anfänger"

- Telepathie für Anfänger (60 S.)
- Telepathie für Fortgeschrittene (52 S.)
- Telekinese für Anfänger (52 S.)
- Lebenskraft für Anfänger (60 S.)
- Meditation für Anfänger (56 S.)
- Kundalini für Anfänger (100 S.)
- Hypnose für Anfänger (56 S.)
- Auto-Movement für Anfänger (56 S.)
- Chakra-Magie für Anfänger (148 S.)
- Astralreisen für Anfänger (56 S.)
- Astrologie für Anfänger (120 S.)
- Ritual-Magie für Anfänger (56 S.)
- Mandalas für Anfänger (68 S.)
- Geldzauber für Anfänger (56 S.)
- Liebeszauber für Anfänger (52 S.)
- Invokationen für Anfänger (52 S.)
- Evokationen für Anfänger (60 S.)
- Elfen für Anfänger (56 S.)
- Magie-Forschung für Anfänger (140 S.)
- Selbsterkenntnis für Anfänger (52 S.)
- Zahlensymbolik für Anfänger (60 S.)
- Die Sprache des Mondes – für Anfänger (116 S.)
- Zaubergesänge für Anfänger (100 S.)
- Zukunftschau für Anfänger (60 S.)
- Schamanismus für Anfänger (52 S.)
- Magische Gegenstände für Anfänger (68 S.)
- Da'ath-Magie für Anfänger (64 S.)
- Kornkreise für Anfänger (348 S.)
- Feng Shui für Anfänger (96 S.)
- Magie für Anfänger – Sammelband I (696 S.)
- Magie für Anfänger – Sammelband II (664 S.)
- Magie für Anfänger – Sammelband III (580 S.)

„Traumreisen"

- Traumreisen zu Heilpflanzen (700 S.)

Magie

- Handbuch für Zauberlehrlinge (408 S.)
- Tarot (104 S.)
- Physik und Magie (184 S.)
- Die Synthese von Physik und Magie (200S.)
- Die Magie-Formel (156 S.)
- Krafttiere – Tiergöttinnen – Tiertänze (112 S.)
- Schwitzhütten (524 S.)
- Mythen und Magie der Harfe (116 S.)
- Magie heute – Berichte aus der Praxis (288 S.)

Meditation

- Der Lebenskraftkörper (230 S.)
- Die Chakren (100 S.)
- Das Chakren-System mit den Nebenchakren (296 S.)
- Organe und Chakren (64 S.)
- Die platonischen Körper in den Chakren (156 S.)
- Meditation (140 S.)
- Drachenfeuer (124 S.)
- Kundalini I (676 S.)
- Reinkarnation (156 S.)
- einsgerichtet (140 S.)

Astrologie

- Astrologie (496 S.)
- Photo-Astrologie (428 S.)
- Die astrologischen Aspekte (88 S.)
- Horoskop und Seele (120 S.)

Kabbala

- Kursus der praktischen Kabbala (150 S.)
- Eltern der Erde (450 S.)
- Blüten des Lebensbaumes:
    - Die Struktur des kabbalistischen Lebensbaumes (370 S.)
    - Der kabbalistische Lebensbaum als Forschungshilfsmittel (580 S.)
    - Der kabbalistische Lebensbaum als spirituelle Landkarte (520 S.)

Die Themen der 87 Bände der Reihe „Die Götter der Germanen"